101 Way Promote Your Business Opportunity

MW01204845

The information you need to Succeed in
any Home-Based Business!

Ginny Dye

Together We Can Change The World Publishing
Bellingham, WA 98229

Author's Note:

No matter what Business Opportunity you are promoting, your biggest question is, "How do I get people to join my Team?" It's a logical question since your whole success depends on it!

In addition to my own 10 years in Business Building – my last Team having over 160,000 people – I have worked with over 75 other business builders from every company in the industry to compile this list of ideas for you.

Of course, an idea is only as good as the ACTION you take to make it happen... I encourage you to take one idea a day and DO IT. Some of them will work for you – some of them may not. The thing to understand is that if you take consistent action, you will see your Team grow.

As a bonus, you will receive Success Secrets & Stories that will propel you to your dreams if you put them into action.

Yeah – action is pretty important through this book so get ready to be challenged a lot! ☺

Use this Success Workbook the way it is designed and it will CHANGE YOUR LIFE!! Don't shortcut anything. Take it one step at a time and watch your business transform.

With you for Success!

Ginny Dye

Table of Contents

> I hope you're ready for an amazing Journey of exploration, discovery & challenge!

101+ Ways to Promote Your Business Opportunity!

*The first set of ideas cost nothing
but time and effort.*

1) Print Invitations and Flyers and hand them out in your neighborhood. Be sure to include your phone number and address so people can call and talk to you about your Business Opportunity (Biz Op). Take them when traveling, visiting, and wherever you go! *(Most businesses have invitations and flyers you can use, but you may have to create your own.)*

Date, Action & Results

_____

_____

_____

_____

_____

2) Use Yahoo Groups and Google groups where you can find like-minded people who might be interested in your Biz Op. There are a lot of people out there looking for an opportunity and this is free advertising. *(Just do a Google search on Yahoo Groups and Google Groups.*

Date, Action & Results

_____

_____

_____

_____

_____

3) Word of mouth (friends, family, co-workers, etc.) is one of the very best ways to promote your Biz Op. Listen for needs people may have that your business can address. When you talk about your Biz Op start out with a positive experience you've had: "I received a free mall with over a 1000 stores in it that saves me time and money." Or tell about an excellent purchase – even show it off – that you made through your business. Then share some information about your business, send them to the website or invite them to a call.

Date, Action & Results

_____

_____

_____

_____

4) Best results are by making personal contact. Join an online community like AdlandPro and take advantage of their free offers. Send a request to other members that have similar interests and ask them to "be your friend." Most will accept your invitation, then send another message and tell them about your Biz Op.

Date, Action & Results

_____

_____

_____

_____

_____

POWER MODULE # 1

Why Did You Start A Business?

As you move forward in creating financial freedom through your own business it's important to understand - REALLY understand - what brought you into your business in the first place. I'm sure your business has great products, an incredible business system, and tremendous tools for your success. All of those are critically important distinctions, but it's NOT why you decided to build a business of your own.

You decided to jump into a home-based business for a very personal reason. The reasons are as different as the people making the decision. You want to have financial freedom; you're a mom who wants to stay home with your kids; you're a college kid who wants to graduate without educational debts; you're retired and want more than you have now; you want to spend more time with your family... we could go on and on, but I think you have the picture.

The question is; do you yourself know WHY you started a business? It's important! A key part of the process of achieving success in your new business endeavor is knowing what you want.

And yes, this is where we're going to spend some time talking about goals. You may have done this before. But did you do it right? Have you achieved all your goals? If not, hang with me and let's take another stab at this!

Goals will be <u>key</u> to your success. The unconscious mind is constantly processing information in such a way as to move us in particular directions. Even at the unconscious level, the mind is distorting, deleting, and generalizing. What that means is that before the mind can work efficiently, we must fully understand the outcomes we expect to reach. When the mind has a defined target, it can focus and direct and refocus and redirect until it reaches its intended goal. If it doesn't have a defined target, its energy is squandered. It's like the person with the world's fastest speedboat who has no idea why he's sitting in the middle of the ocean!

Setting your goals within your new business is imperative!! Have you ever tried to put together a jigsaw puzzle without having seen the picture of what it represents? That's what happens when you try to build a business without knowing your outcomes. When you know your outcome, you give your brain a clear picture of what it needs to be effective – so you don't waste energy.

Here's one thing to plant firmly in your mind. **<u>Results are inevitable.</u>** If you don't provide your mind with programming for success – someone else will program it with something else. If you don't have your own plan, someone else is going to make you fit into their plan. I don't know about you, but that's just not very appealing to me. I like being in charge of my own life.

Okay, let's get started with this... The following exercise is adapted from Anthony Robbin's book <u>Unlimited Power.</u> I highly recommend it. I encourage you to become a student of both business and successful living. How you approach your business at every stage will be a good indicator of where you are going to take it in the future. I want to help you achieve your highest success. So read on...

Follow these 5 rules in formulating your goals:

1- State your goal in positive terms. Say what you <u>want </u>to happen, not what you don't want to happen. Don't say, "Well, I don't want to be poor anymore." You just programmed POOR into your mind. Instead, say, "I want to be Financially Free – making at least $200,000 a year." Your mind will now work to achieve the goal of what you WANT.

2- Be as specific as possible. Engage all your senses in describing your outcome. Also, be certain to set a specific completion date.

3- Have an evidence procedure. You can be winning and feel like you're losing if you don't keep score.

4- Be in control. Your goal must be initiated and maintained by you - not be dependent upon other people's actions or non-actions.

5- Verify that your goal is ecologically sound and desirable. Simply put, make sure it is one that benefits you and other people.

Take some time now to create your life as you want it to be. Create your business as you want it to be. I realize you are taking time away from "sharing the business," but this is honestly the best use of your time right now. You're taking this time to share your complete vision of your business with your subconscious mind - the part of you that will carry you to success. So set aside some time and walk through what follows. It could be the best time spent with your new business. This book is also meant to be your "Journal to Success" so make sure you take advantage of it. It will become your "Road Map to Success" and will become a treasured part of your life.

1 -**Start by making an inventory of your dreams** - the things you want to have, do, be and share. Don't try to define how you're going to accomplish it now. Just write it down. There are no limits. Don't move on until you have made your list. Make it extensive! Remember, you're creating your life here.

_____

_____

_____

_____

_____

_____

_____

_____

_____

_____

_____

_____

_____

_____

_____

_____

_____

_____

_____

_____

2- Go over the list you made (1 at a time), and then estimate when you expect to reach those outcomes. Six months, one year, two years, five years, ten years, twenty years. A journey of a thousand miles begins with one step. It's important to be aware of the both the first steps and the final ones.

3- Pick out the four most important goals for you this year. Write down why you absolutely will achieve them. Be clear, concise and positive. Tell yourself why you're sure you can reach those outcomes, and why it's important that you do. If you can find enough reasons to do something, you can get yourself to do anything. Reasons are the difference between being interested in something versus being committed to accomplishing something. If you get a big enough why, you can always figure out the how.

_____

_____

_____

_____

_____

4- Now that you have a list of your key goals, review them against the five rules for formulating outcomes (the 5 we gave you above). Change any that you need to fit.

_____

_____

_____

_____

_____

_____

_____

_____

_____

_____

_____

_____

_____

_____

_____

_____

5- Make a list of the important resources you already have at hand.
Make a list of what you have going for you: character traits, friends, financial resources, education, time, energy, or whatever.

_____

_____

_____

_____

_____

_____

_____

_____

_____

_____

_____

_____

_____

_____

_____

_____

6- When you've done that, focus in on times you used some of those resources most skillfully. It can be anything from a killing on the stock market to a wonderful day with your kids. Describe what you did that made you succeed, what qualities or resources you made effective use of, and what about that situation made you feel successful.

_____

_____

_____

_____

_____

_____

_____

_____

_____

_____

_____

_____

_____

_____

7- Now describe what kind of person you will have to be to attain your goals. We hear a lot about success, but we don't hear as much about the components of success - the attitudes, beliefs, and behaviors that go into producing it. If you don't have a good grasp of the components, you may find it difficult to put together the whole, so stop now and write a couple of paragraphs or a page about all the character traits, skills, attitudes, beliefs and disciplines you will need to have as a person to achieve all that you desire.

_____

_____

_____

_____

_____

_____

_____

_____

_____

_____

_____

_____

_____

8- Write down what prevents you from having the things you want right now. We all have ways of limiting ourselves, our own strategies for failing, but by recognizing your past limitation strategies, you can change them now.

_____

_____

_____

_____

_____

_____

_____

_____

_____

_____

_____

_____

_____

We can know what we want, why we want it, who will help us, and a lot of other things, but the critical ingredient that in the end determines whether we succeed in achieving our outcomes is our actions. We must create a step by step plan. What are the necessary actions you must take consistently to produce the results you desire?

9- Take the time now to take each of your four key goals and create your first draft of a step-by-step plan on how to achieve it. Make sure your plans include something you can do TODAY!

_____

_____

_____

_____

_____

_____

_____

_____

_____

_____

_____

_____

10 - What's the surest way to achieve excellence? It's to model someone who has already done what you want to do. So come up with some models. You can save time and energy, and avoid traveling down wrong paths by following the example of people who've succeeded already. Come up with the models for all the areas of your life you want to change now. (This book has many stories of people who can become models, but you may already have your own list.)

_____

_____

_____

_____

_____

_____

_____

_____

_____

_____

_____

_____

_____

_____

I sincerely hope you have done all that is included here. Please don't take this lightly. Preparing your mind and heart are the first crucial steps in having a successful home-based business!

Now, because if you're like me, you've had some additional thoughts and ideas – please write them down here. You'll be so glad you have this in the future!

_____

_____

_____

_____

_____

_____

_____

_____

_____

_____

It has been said that there are only two pains in life - the pain of discipline or the pain of regret. Discipline weighs ounces. Regret weighs tons.

POWER STORY # 1

ONE-LEGGED BASKETBALL PLAYER

14 year old Mark Haley was already a basketball star. He had broken every scoring record at his school and was on his way to becoming a legend. *That was before...*

...before the accident. He was with 4 of his friends – heading into town for a night at the movies. They were all laughing and talking when the car hit an icy patch, spun out of control, and slammed into the guardrail. Mark was catapulted from the rear window. When the state patrol arrived, Mark was sitting on the side of the road, staring at a torrent of blood gushing from his right thigh. His right leg, severed through by a guardrail cable, was just five feet away.

Surgery saved his life but it couldn't save his leg. Mark's first words were, "What about my basketball career?" He already had big plans for playing college ball, then becoming a pro. The doctors exchanged looks but didn't have an answer for him.

When he found out his coach and team were in the waiting room he sent a message. "Tell Coach I'll be back next year." No one dared defy him but only his parents believed he had a chance to do it.

Mark knew from the beginning that his attitude was everything. "I'm not going to feel sorry for myself. I don't really see where that can help." And, "Instead of being bitter and angry, I'm just going to be positive." When he sensed pity from people, his response was always the same. "Don't feel bad for me. I'll be just fine." Then he set out to prove it.

When he returned home his life was physical therapy and tutoring to keep up with his school work. He pushed himself in therapy, ignoring the pain and driving hard to regain his strength and balance. One afternoon, when no one was home, he hobbled out back to the basketball court. He put down his crutches, started hopping on one leg, and began to shoot hoops. Within seconds he lost his balance and crashed to the asphalt. He picked himself up and started again. 15 minutes later he was exhausted, but not defeated.

I guess this is going to take a little longer than I thought...

4 months after the accident he got his first prosthesis. He thought it would make things easier. In fact, it was harder. He drove himself to learn how to walk with his prosthetic leg, then shoot the basketball, then run. His doctors suspected it would be at least a year before he would even walk comfortably with his new leg. They didn't know Mark.

I'm going to have to work even harder. I just can't give up.

Slowly he got better but whenever he tried to push himself on the basketball court, he usually just crashed to the ground. The thought came to him that maybe he just couldn't do it, but he just as quickly pushed it down. He just had to work harder. He began a daily regimen of shooting, dribbling and weight lifting. The effort left huge blisters on his leg from the prosthetic but he ignored it and pushed on – buoyed by the knowledge he was making progress. What was a little pain?

That fall, against all odds, Mark Haley made the basketball team. And he made it, secure in the knowledge he had earned it. No one had worked harder than he had during tryouts. The whole team cheered when he was elected team captain.

His first game started out as a disaster. He was jerky and awkward, shooting off balance, and throwing up air balls. His rhythm was totally off. The coach called him out for a breather, then put him back in with just a few minutes left in the half. *Come on, Mark. This is what you've worked for. Show them you can do it!* Seconds later he worked himself free, received a pass, and put up a long 3-pointer. The stands erupted. Then he drove to the basket, pulled down a rebound, and muscled it back up to the board, scoring again.

Mark was back.

Mark chose to turn what could have been a disaster into a victory. He determined to be positive and to do whatever it took to accomplish his goals. He went on to play high school basketball and tennis. He is now a college basketball coach. No one on his team ever makes excuses – they wouldn't dare. Not a one of them has to play with one leg.

Everyone has limitations. Everyone has problems. Everyone has things in their life that stands as an obstacle to reaching their dreams. The ones who succeed are the ones who decide to. Who decide to not let anything stop them. Who decide to do whatever it takes to make their dreams come true. You can do that, too.

5) If you have a personal website, write about your Biz Op and put banners or information there! Some email clients host one page for you free. Use it!

Date, Action & Results

_____

_____

_____

_____

_____

_____

6) Any time you hear people talking, listen for an open door. It can be anything about money, jobs, shopping, etc. so you can step up and invite them check out a way to make money. Hand them your Invitation Card or Business Card with your domain name or Biz Op URL on it. Don't answer any questions, tell them it's all there for them to explore. This takes the pressure off of them since you aren't trying to sell them anything.

Date, Action & Results

_____

_____

_____

_____

_____

_____

7) Place free classified ads with your local online paper and college paper. People are always looking for a way to make money and you might just get some people interested enough to take a look at your Biz Op.

Date, Action & Results

_____

_____

_____

_____

_____

_____

8) You're looking for Entrepreneurs. Ask, "Did you have a lemonade stand as a kid? Sell candy bars? Cut grass?" If they were entrepreneurial that far back, it's still in them!

Date, Action & Results

_____

_____

_____

_____

_____

_____

_____

POWER MODULE # 2

You Want To Know This Law!

There is one single LAW you will want to understand as you build your business. It will not only help your business – it will transform every area of your life if you use it. It's called the **Law of Attraction**, one of many Universal Laws.

Universal Laws govern the Universe. They are basic principles of life and have been around since Creation. They are laws of the Divine Universe. Universal Laws apply to everyone - everywhere. They cannot be changed. They cannot be broken.

The Universal Law of Attraction (LOA) is the most powerful force in the universe. It is simple in concept but practice is necessary. However, once you "get it", there is no looking back! It will be part of you forever. The simplest definition of this law is "like attracts like." Other definitions include:
*   *You get what you think about, whether wanted or unwanted.*
*   *All forms of matter and energy are attracted to that which is of a like vibration.*
*   *You are a living magnet.*
*   *You get what you put your energy and focus on, whether wanted or unwanted.*
*   *Energy attracts like energy.*
*   *Everything draws to itself that which is like itself.*
Here are some ways of expressing the Law of Attraction:
*   *Birds of a feather flock together*
*   *Like attracts like*
*   *Whatever you want wants you*
*   *What you sow, you reap*
*   *What you put out you get back*
*   *What comes around goes around*

The Law of Attraction is fun to learn and use because you are always watching, waiting expectantly for your desires to manifest. You can deliberately use this law to create your future!

This universal law is working in your life right now, whether you are aware of it or not. You are attracting people, situations, jobs and much more into your life. Whether you know it or not, you attracted your Biz Op into your life.

26

Once you are aware of this law and how it works, you can start to use it to deliberately attract what you want into your life – including people into your business!

How do you create your desires using this powerful law? There are just a few basic steps.

1. Get very clear on what you want. It's important to know what you WANT; not what you *don't* want. For instance, you don't want to say, "Well, I don't want to be poor." You want to say, "I want to be financially free, creating $_____ per month."

2. Visualize what you want. Choose to feel POSITIVE about what you are visualizing. Your mind will work harder to support those things you feel good about.

3. Allow It. Allow what you want to come to you by "yes'ing" your way through life. **'Just Say Yes'** to abundance. **'Just Say Yes'** to great relationships. **'Just Say Yes'** to a healthy body. **'Just Say Yes'** to work that you love. Get the picture? Your job is to simply identify what you want, get into the place where you can actually feel what it will be like having it, and then allow it to flow to you by holding your focus there.

4. Take inspired action. The Universe will open ways for you to achieve what you want. Let's say you want 20 Biz Op reps in your first month. You get clear on what you want; you visualize it happening, and you say YES to it. If your focus is there, the Universe will make the way. You'll run into just the right people. You'll decide to do something within these Training Letters that has great results. Or you'll think of something totally new that brings you what you want!

You must be very clear on exactly what your desire is. Focus on it. Give it all your positive energy. Feel good!

A major factor behind this Universal Law is the energy and vibrations of our emotions and feelings. Any thought you may have, when combined with emotion, vibrates out from you to the universe and will attract back what you want.

You can leave all the details to the universe. Let the Universe figure out the method of delivery, when you will receive it, etc. Now all you have to do is "Allow It." Sounds easy, right? This can be the most difficult part to do. Be doubt-free. All you need to do is expect it. Act like you already have it. Be grateful.

And always TAKE INSPIRED ATION. If something feels right, then go ahead and do it. Taking action is an important step. You can visualize a blue Cadillac but it isn't going to fall out of the sky. You still have to take action to get it!

That is it! You can always be expectant of good things, your desires. Feel good knowing your desire is on its way to you.

Always expect your desires. Expect miracles.

How can you apply the Law of Attraction RIGHT NOW?

_____

_____

_____

_____

_____

_____

_____

_____

_____

_____

POWER STORY # 2

I can just imagine James's elation when his book *Breaking Back: How I Lost Everything and Won Back My Life,* hit the New York bestseller list. If it had been me, disbelief and thankfulness would have overwhelmed me. Many sports players have a "story" to tell, and James Blake is no exception. If you followed the U.S. Tennis team's progress in the 2008 Beijing Olympics, you will remember James as part of that team - he was one of the three men's singles players. However, before we jump ahead to his accomplishments, let's look at what this young sports star has overcome in order to stand in the winner's circle.

Imagine a junior high school athlete standing in the doctor's office learning about a back condition called scoliosis. The condition required him to wear a full-length back brace *18 hours a day for five years to help straighten his spine.*

Imagine a Harvard University student dropping out after his sophomore year in order to play professional tennis.

Imagine rising to the top of the tennis world and coming out to practice. Running toward the net, he slips, falls, and hears a sickening crack – his neck is broken. With a broken back and crushed vertebra, he is sidelined from competing – with little hope of recovery.

Imagine (in the same year) receiving a phone call that your father is dying of stomach cancer.

Imagine (again in the same year) contracting shingles, suffering facial paralysis, and severely blurred vision.

Imagine later, the incredible reality of being named the 2005 Association of Tennis Professionals Comeback Player of the Year.

Imagine being named one of America's Sexiest Men.

Imagine becoming the first man in years with African-American heritage to break into Tennis's Top 10.

These events, plus many more, comprise the life of James Blake. Major events such as cancer and a broken back compound his every win and every loss into personal victories and setbacks.

What does a young man do when his dream is to play tennis? What does he do when his life requires him to start all over again?

Well, if you are James, you keep starting over until you succeed. When disaster returns to knock you down again, you get up and keep trying.

You and I should apply this same advice to our lives. Regardless of our ages, we have events in life that sideline us. We also endure times where major drama and trauma cripple us. Instead of giving in to these events, be like James and attempt to be the "comeback player of the year."

Whenever you get discouraged, remember James' story of determination, stamina, and endurance. If he can make such a dramatic comeback, I know you and I can too.

When the world says, "Give Up,"

Hope whispers, "Try it one more time..."

9) Email all your business contacts, especially those you know have a desire to start a business, already own a business, or are business minded. (Don't exclude ANYONE, but start with your business contacts.) Start off by sending out a little note asking permission to send them information about an exciting new concept you've discovered.

Date, Action & Results

_____

_____

_____

_____

_____

_____

_____

_____

10) Share your Biz Op by sending a "reply" to all of your incoming email including spam. Write up a compelling email that will get people to take a look. You don't want to beat them over the head, and you don't want to bore them to death. Here's one I saw recently that had a powerful response. _Your Biz Op won't have the same features, but it should give you some ideas..._

Hello _____,

Okay, I'm totally surprised... After swearing to never again look at a home-based business, I finally agreed to just take a look after someone sent me 5 emails - just to get them off my back and show them all the reasons it wouldn't work!   That's when I discovered the ██████████

* It's totally FR`EE. Really!

* You don't ever have to Se`ll anything. Really!

* You don't ever have to Bu`y anything. Really!

* It's the most simple concept I've ever seen. I think that is its power. I just installed a toolbar on my computer, take 5 minutes a day to click on some links, and I'm done!

* You don't have to train anyone. It's really so simple that anyone can do it!

They say you can make $43,000 in one month. I don't know if you can or not, but I like the amount I've made in the last few days! Can you think of at least 5 people who would like what I just described? You ought to at least take a look!

Just use this link to check it out yourself! It will take you 4 minutes and 42 seconds to decide if it's for you. You just might be as surprised as I am!

█████████████

Date, Action & Results

_____

_____

_____

_____

_____

_____

_____

_____

_____

_____

_____

11) Don't try to reinvent the wheel. Use the tools available. When you're out and about, pass out invitation cards or flyers to cashiers at the grocery store or the "bag boy." Do this everywhere you go: sporting events, restaurants, the beach, chamber of commerce after hours business card exchanges or breakfasts, the movie theater, literally everywhere you go. Just hand them a business card or flyer.

Date, Action & Results

_____

_____

_____

_____

12) Create a welcome email for everyone who signs up under you. Include advertising information (free and paid) along with links to helpful articles. Include your Instant Messenger ID so they can reach you faster than email. ☐ *(If you don't know about Instant Messenger, just go to www.Hotmail.com or www.Yahoo.com . It's easy to get started.)*

Date, Action & Results

_____

_____

_____

_____

POWER MODULE # 3

The Magic of Doubling

Right here, as you begin to build your business, I want to make sure you don't get sucked into the Get Rich Quick Mentality that can make you walk away from a great business opportunity before you have given it enough time to work for you. I encourage you to start your home-based business with a "2 Year Mentality". Choose to give it your all for 2 years, building steadily on a daily basis. If you commit to that you will achieve the Financial Freedom you dream of!

Let's play with some numbers...

Let's say you've been working your business hard for a couple months, you've built a good foundation, and your first check is $40. You think, "Oh man, is this thing going to work?" *You're already thinking about quitting...*

Let's take a look at the "Magic of Doubling". Let's say that your checks just double each month for 1 year. Is that a number you can wrap your brain around? Your team will continue to grow, and you will continue to put as many people on your frontline as possible. If you agree you're going to do these things, let's take a look at what is possible:

Month 1 Payment: $40

Month 2 Payment: $80

Month 3 Payment: $160

Month 4 Payment: $320

Month 5 Payment: $640

Month 6 Payment: $1280

Month 7 Payment: $2560

Month 8 Payment: $5120

Month 9 Payment: $10,240

Month 10 Payment: $20,480

Month 11 Payment: $40,960

Month 12 Payment: $81,920

The first time I did this my eyes grew really wide... :)

Too many of us are looking for the "Get Rich Quick Scheme" that is going to work this time. Folks, such a thing really doesn't exist. Oh, when a new thing comes along there will always be a few people who get rich quickly - and then they'll get richer by convincing you that you can do the same thing, and then selling you that information. The Internet is full of those kinds of schemes - that's why so many people have gotten burnt.

Any business will take time, persistence and dedication in order to achieve your goals. Some of you will explode quickly - Great! Others of you will grow slow and steady - Great! Both ways are wonderful. Both ways will get you to where you want to go.

What are your "Doubling Goals"?

Month 1   _____

Month 2   _____

Month 3   _____

Month 4   _____

Month 5   _____

Month 6   _____

Month 7   _____

Month 8   _____

Month 9   _____

Month 10   _____

Month 11   _____

Month 12   _____

What are you going to

do TODAY

to create

FINANCIAL

INDEPENDENCE

for yourself?

I turned the slick paper and studied the glossy 5x7 photo of the *"13th Most Powerful Woman of the U.S. OVER the age of 80."* Wondering who she happened to be, I studied her long legs and relentless countenance.

So far, she seemed fairly tame. Aside from several struggles with secretarial jobs, not much grabbed my attention. I felt sorry for her losses. Yet one question rambled around in my mind.

Why was she so powerful? And rich? What had this woman accomplished that landed her on the list of the top most powerful women in the U.S.?

Reading excerpts of her life, the job as a swanky, edgy magazine editor dimmed.

She had known heartache. She had experienced trouble. In addition, she experienced much controversy. Yet seeing her past in print led to a deeper understanding of her present. I let my eyes move off her face and scroll down to her biography.

- *Born in 1922 in Arkansas, U.S.A. to a schoolteacher father and homemaker mother.*

- *Her father died an accident when she was 10.*

- *Her older sister developed polio and suffered paralysis.*

- *Her mother lived in deep depression and sadness.*

- *She left home, and reinvented herself to avoid the poverty-stricken future she feared.*

- *In 7 years she held 18 different secretarial jobs.*

- *Married in 1959 for the first and only time at the age of 37.*

- *Published her first book at age 40, highlighting her life as a single woman.*

Turning the next page, I understood who I held in my hand.

This woman, age 86, recently "retired" as the editor-in-chief of COSMOPOLITAN magazine.

Helen Gurley Brown had served 32 years at the helm of the magazine. When she took over, it had a measly 800,000 subscriptions. She took it to the top! Now in more than 27 countries, this woman's magazine stormed the publishing industry with over 3 million subscriptions. It remains the sixth best-selling newsstand magazine in any category. While she left the American version of COSMOPOLITAN, she remains editor-in-chief of their INTERNATIONAL versions...all 59 of them!

If you read about her life or simply read her magazine, you quickly see both are teeming with controversial and risqué exploits. Gurley says, *"A million times a year I defend my covers....I like skin, I like pretty. I didn't want to photograph the girl next door."*

Gurley does not "settle" for anything yet more than half a dozen literary awards have been bestowed on her.

She's a published author 8 - times.

Her yearly salary? An estimated $50 million!

She and her husband share a Central Park penthouse apartment. (He is a successful movie producer.)

Of her life and about life in general she says:

- *"I never liked the looks of the life that was programmed for me - ordinary, hillbilly, and poor."*
- *"Beauty can't amuse you, but brainwork - reading, writing, thinking - can."*
- *"People think chutzpah is in the genes. It isn't...it's in the needing and wanting and being willing to fall on your face. It isn't fun...who wants all that rejection, but life is sweeter if you make yourself do uncomfortable things."*
- *"Money, if it does not bring you happiness, will at least help you be miserable in comfort."*
- Her advice on being a good executive: *"Pay a compliment before criticizing someone, say 'no' to time wasters, do what you dread first, and work harder than anybody else."*

Gurley should know. At age 86, she works 5-6 days a week, exercises faithfully twice a day, abstains from coffee and tea, and attends a weekly dance class with her husband. She scrutinizes her fat and protein intake and *leaps* to answer the phone in her stiletto heels! In an interview several years ago, when asked if she regretted the era she grew up in, this is how she answered:

"How many people are there like me (who are 81) still making a ton of money, with a wonderful job? To say I would prefer to be a 21-year-old now would be absolutely insane."

Well, whatever one thinks of her...her life has been anything but dull and routine. She started her career with a sickly sister and an emotionally fragile mom. She made a life for all of them - not without criticism and critique, but a life nonetheless, and she carved it out herself.

I so hope that at 86 years of age, I too, am still doing it my way. Oh, I doubt I'll oversee trend-setting, contentious magazines...yet I do want to live life on my own terms.

I hope you caught Gurney's quote, "*...life is sweeter if you make yourself do uncomfortable things.*"

Sometimes we do go through uncomfortable situations before we reach sweeter times. It is never fun, but oftentimes it is through the struggle that we find we possess the strength to succeed. If you are in the midst of "uncomfortable things," then hang on...it will get better. Just don't give up!

I hope you will persevere like Helen Gurley Brown and develop your own lifestyle.

Dare to be different and dare to be unique. That is what makes the world go around, ya know!

> "*...life is sweeter if you make yourself do uncomfortable things.*"

13) When you send out an invitation via email give just enough information to get people curious. Always include a link to your Biz Op site. Send invitations out about every two weeks. Realize this may be simple, but it isn't easy. However the long term benefits are good. Have long term goals to keep yourself focused on the positives so you won't get discouraged when people don't sign up.

Date, Action & Results

_____

_____

_____

_____

_____

14) Flyers, flyers, flyers – Your Biz Op should have some you can copy. If not, ask them to create some. They will appreciate your initiative! Keep them in your car, all your bags (or purses), even you kids' school bags because you never know when you'll need them. Hand them out, post them on bulletin boards at schools, supermarkets, hair and nail salons, restaurants, etc. (get permission first).

Date, Action & Results

_____

_____

_____

_____

_____

15) People join people, so develop relationships. It can be as simple as a handshake and a smile, but people will be drawn to your Biz Op because they are drawn to you. Then invite them to your website. Also, once you have people on your team, work with the willing. Don't try to build someone else's business for them, but help those who are trying. You might buy them domain names, show them social networking sites like MySpace.com, Me.com, Yuwie.com, Facebook and others.

Date, Action & Results

_____

_____

_____

_____

16) Write articles about shopping and home and making and saving money, and distribute them through free outlets such as EzineArticles.com and Xomba.com. These articles can include a link to your Biz Op site and they stay active for months to years. You don't have to be a professional writer. All you need is a point of view and a passion to introduce people to the wonderful benefits of having their own business. If you want a powerful way to automate it (this will cost some) just go to www.articleannouncer.com. It's the best I've found!

Date, Action & Results

_____

_____

_____

_____

_____

_____

POWER MODULE # 4

Your Warm Market

You will find the most success with your Warm Market. Warm market? The definition of a warm market is simple; it is a group of individuals from your present and past whom you know well enough that were you to pick up the phone and call them, they would recognize you once they heard your name.

Now, we realize there are some of you out there who are part of the NFL club. (No friends left!) You may have done so many home-based businesses that people run when they see you coming. ☺ Or maybe you just don't have a circle of friends, or you live in the boonies somewhere. That can be a reality, and there are systems to enable you to build a business no matter what your situation is, but we'll concentrate on those later. For now we're going to focus on your warm market. Here's what you want to do.

Make a list of at least 100 people you know. *100?* **Yes, you can do it!** This can be critical to your success. Go through your address book. Think of everybody you come into contact with. What about people at church? At work? In your neighborhood? Who do you know who's good with people? Teachers? People who deal with the public? Go through the yellow pages. You'll be surprised how many people you really know.

We think a good goal is to have your first 10 people come from within your warm market. Expand out from there in any way you want.

Now, here's the thing that should help you relax. You don't have to pick up that phone that suddenly weighs 100 lbs and call them. Remember your flyers, Invitation Cards, Emails, etc? Almost every Biz Op has created them for you. UTILIZE THEM!

Of course, if you're one of those people who doesn't mind talking on the phone, and you actually want to call them, here's all you need to say: *I just got involved with a very exciting opportunity   Do you know anyone that would like to make additional income working part-time from home?"*

When they say "me", or "doing what", or "what company", or any other question, **DO NOT ATTEMPT TO EXPLAIN THE BUSINESS!** *Get their*

email address so you can send them an E-card or email with the link to your Biz Op. Don't just give them your website address – they might not go. If they open an email from you and only have to click on a link, they'll go!

If you're with them in person, hand them an Invitation card or Flyer, or get their Email address.

ALWAYS GET THEIR PHONE NUMBER! Say, "Give me your phone number and I'll call you in a few days to see if you have any questions." Notice: you didn't sell anything. You didn't talk about the company. **THE LESS YOU SAY THE BETTER. DON'T TALK ABOUT THE BUSINESS!**

Why? It's not that you're trying to hide anything. You believe you have the best business opportunity in America, don't you!. But we have learned to let your tools do the work for you. Because they are so well done, and because they do such a great job of presenting the company, you will give your prospects the best possible chance of getting involved. If you think you can do a better job talking to people, you're probably mistaken. And, hey, what's the point of trying to reinvent the wheel? Find a system that works and DO IT!

Let's say for discussion sake that you COULD do an incredible job of talking to people yourself - without using any of the great tools available. You might be the world's greatest sales person. But so what? It's not duplicable. Not many other people are great sales people. You need to do things everyone can do. ANYONE can send out Emails or hand out Invitation Cards. You have to have a system that ANYONE can do if you want your business to succeed. Your success will come as more people join your Team. If people can't duplicate your actions, you have a job, not a business!

Trust me on this one. DON'T EXPLAIN THE BUSINESS!! There - have we made ourselves plain enough? ☺ We hope so, because this is crucial to your success. Give your Biz Op tools to everybody you meet.

A few more key things to remember:

1) Your enthusiasm is what

will convince people to take a look. You don't need to know anything except that you are excited about your Biz Op! That implies a belief level that allows that enthusiasm. If there are lingering doubts, or questions that are hindering you, please call your sponsor and talk through them! Watch your Biz Op movie once a day to remind you just how great it is! ***ATTITUDE IS MORE IMPORTANT THAN ABILITY!***

2) Don't shy away from your warm market, saying *"Well, I'll talk to them when I'm making more money."* Don't you want to make money WITH your friends and family?

The money issue is easily solvable. If they ask you, *"How much money are you making?"* just say, *"Hey, I'm just getting started in this thing! But look at it for yourself. What have you got to lose? I guarantee you it is different from anything you've ever seen before!"*

3) Don't try to sell people on your Biz Op. It is your job to simply share the business and give them all the information to make a sound business decision for themselves. You don't ever want to pressure someone. It's NOT the way we do business! It IS the way to lose all your friends!

You might be able to convince someone intellectually that joining your Biz Op is a great decision, but if that person does not believe they can succeed, or if they do not believe in themselves and their own abilities to learn and grow - all your great salesmanship is useless.

> ***Building a successful Biz Op is a NUMBERS GAME!*** Those who talk to the most people WIN!

POWER STORY # 4

Traveling the road from Iowa to New York City takes a little while. The young, red-haired woman felt her dreams grow as each mile took her farther away from the familiar and closer to her dreams. Thoughts of home tried to squeeze out her anticipation. Shifting her weight, Marcia wondered where home would be in ten years. Wondered who she would know - what she would do. Right now, though, the focus was on getting a job, getting discovered, and seeing her name up in lights.

The memory of Marcia's graduation from college that morning didn't last long. A few hours of celebration and she was out of Iowa. Deeply relieved to leave behind her unhappy childhood, complete with alcoholic and abusive parents, Marcia was finally free and on her own. With more weight (230 lbs) on her body than money ($150) in her pocket, she knew she had better live fast and wisely. (Years later, Marcia advises theatre wannabes, and others starting out, to make sure their dream money at least equals their body weight!)

This dreamy, starry-eyed woman packed her bags and left on the road to pursue her dreams. Happily, she found peace along the way. Marcia continues today to see dreams fulfilled with successful stints in New York and Hollywood - the stage and television.

However, the road to her dreams (and her peace) came littered with more than a few detours.

"Marcia? You applied to substitute teach and we can use you. Can you start on Monday? See you then."

*"Marcia? The job typing scripts is yours. You can start with **Hello Dolly**."*

"Marcia? We need someone to sell bed sheets. Great, you can start tomorrow!"

"Marcia? You cannot yell "shuto upo" to the Spanish students. Please take your things as you leave."

"The Emmy nomination goes to Marcia Wallace!"

"The Emmy goes to Marcia Wallace!"

It is easy to look at Marcia and just notice her *pages* of acting, television, animation, Broadway, theatre, Hollywood, game show, and comedy club credits and think, "Wow! Look at where she is."

However, if you look a bit deeper, you realize that more accurately, the thought is "Wow, look how far she has come!" If you still can't place Marcia, think back to the zany, red-headed receptionist on the *Bob Newhart Show*, with Bob Newhart and Suzanne Pleshette that ran in the 1970's! Or remember the voice of Edna Krabapple on the Simpsons - that is Marcia.

Marcia is also a breast cancer survivor, a rape victim, a widow, had her

house burn down, lost 100 pounds, is a single mom, suffered a nervous breakdown with a stay at a psychiatric unit (she calls it "the bin"), and survived menopause!

Her newest endeavor is author, and you've gotta love the name of her book: *Don't Look Back, We're Not Going That Way* with the greatest subtitle, *How I Overcame a Rocky Childhood, a Nervous Breakdown, Breast Cancer, Widowhood, Fat, Fire & Menopausal Motherhood and Still Managed to Count My Lucky Chickens.*

WOW! Today when I look forward to seeing my dreams fulfilled, I hope I have as much grace, forgiveness and "stick-to-it-tive-ness" as Marcia. I know we all have (and will have) our own obstacles. Remember Marci as you step out in pursuit of your dreams.

And if life is hard, then go rent an old episode of the Bob Newhart Show. You know, laughter is the best medicine for all that ails you!

Keep on dreaming and reaching for the stars.

 **17) Slide a business card part way into the credit/debit slot of the gas pump.** Most gas stations now have outdoor "credit card" machines in the pumps. So the next person who comes along will remove your business card and have it in hand in order to insert their credit or gas card.

Date, Action & Results

_____

_____

_____

_____

18) Join lots of networking sites. This is time consuming, but as you cultivate online friendships, people take you seriously. Share your positive experiences with your Biz Op. DirectMatches is an online "matchmaking system" that helps people locate everything from business contacts to job opportunities to dating by connecting people who are actively looking for what you might have.

Date, Action & Results

_____

_____

_____

_____

_____

_____

19) Be yourself. Don't try to pretend you know it all. If you believe in your Biz Op people will catch your enthusiasm. Duplicate – duplicate. The site given to you is what you show people. You don't have to know everything or answer questions. Read everything your Biz Op provides you over and over again. Don't expect others to hold your hand. Initiative is what will get you moving forward. Rome wasn't built in a day and neither is a solid business. Set goals and do what it takes to reach them.

Date, Action & Results

_____

_____

_____

_____

_____

20) If English is a second language for you, translate portions of the website, the business cards, Invitation Cards, and other BIZ OP resources and send to others who speak your language.

Date, Action & Results

_____

_____

_____

_____

_____

_____

_____

POWER MODULE # 5

Do You Have Your List?

So... did you make your list of 100 people? If you did – Congratulations! If not, it's time to make it!

The Actions you take today will determine the rest of your life!

All I'm going to do in this Power Module is give you some memory joggers.

Who do you know who...

You respect; shows genuine concern for other people; is active in their church; people always seem to like; does personal counseling; is a professional; is in clubs and various group organizations or active in civic affairs; is in a teaching position in a school or business; deals with the public (such as police officers, firefighters, mail carriers, city officials); is in a management, supervisory, consultant, or trainer capacity; is looking for more out of life; is ambitious, assertive, and "on the go", is considered a leader; attracts leaders; has children just starting junior high, high school, or college; has children with special talents that need to be developed; wants to set a good example for their children to follow; owns a business; holds a very responsible position that is causing stress and pressure; wants to have freedom; is considering a new profession, changing jobs, or has recently changed jobs; is unable to advance in her job; has talents but is held back; just started selling or is an experienced direct salesperson; relies on ideas for his livelihood (authors, designers, promoters, advertisers); has never been able to get started or failed in business but still has strong desires; is going to college, business school, trade school, etc., or just graduated; was recently married and is just "starting out"; knows everyone in town; has international connections; exudes credibility; is elected to office; works with you now; you see at the gym; is looking for a job; you play tennis with; you know from the old neighborhood; appraised your home; already has a great job; takes care of your car; is on your Christmas card list; you take your cleaning to; is your accountant; you do civic work with; does your hair; runs the spa; you see at the copy shop; delivers your mail; seems to change jobs often; did your home repairs; is into sports fitness; wants more time with the family.

_____

_____

_____

_____

_____

_____

_____

_____

_____

_____

_____

_____

_____

_____

_____

_____

Who are your Relatives:

Parents, grandparents, sisters, brothers, aunts, uncles, cousins, children, step-relations...

_____

_____

_____

_____

_____

_____

_____

Who is your...

Mail carrier, newspaper deliverer, dentist, physician, minister, florist, lawyer, insurance agent, accountant, congressional representative, pharmacist, veterinarian, optometrist?

_____

_____

_____

_____

_____

_____

_____

_____

Who sold you your...

House, car/tires, television/stereo, fishing license, hunting license, suit, tie, shoes, business cards, wedding rings, eyeglasses/contacts, vacuum cleaner, boat, camper, motorcycle, bicycle, living room furniture, air conditioner, kitchen appliances, lawnmower, luggage, Avon products, Tupperware, carpet?

_____

_____

_____

_____

_____

_____

_____

_____

_____

Do you know someone who...

Lives next door/across the street; is my spouse's barber/hairdresser; teaches your children at school; was best man/usher/maid of honor/bridesmaid; was the photographer who took your wedding pictures; is the purchasing agent where you work; is the finance director at school; goes hunting or fishing with you; was your Army/Navy buddy; is the architect who drew up house plans; goes bowling with you; is president of the PTA; was your college fraternity brother/sorority sister; you met camping; is the credit manager of the store where you shop; is your spouse's old high school teacher/principal; repaired your television; upholstered your couch; you knew from your old job; went with you to the races; is in your car pool, installed your telephone; has a Laundromat; teaches ceramics; owns a taxi service; cuts the grass; painted the house; owns the pet store where you bought your pet; installed your refrigerator; renewed your driver's license; owns an apartment; is in Rotary/Lions/Kiwanis with you; is Jaycee president; plays bridge with you; is in garden club; book club; is my child's kindergarten teacher; is a deacon in your church;

_____

_____

_____

_____

_____

_____

_____

_____

_____

_____

_____

_____

_____

_____

_____

_____

_____

_____

_____

_____

_____

_____

_____

_____

Who do you know who is a professional...

Now is the time to open your yellow pages and go through every section. Who do you know who works in the fields and areas you find there? Add them to your list...

_____

_____

_____

_____

_____

_____

_____

_____

_____

_____

_____

_____

DO IT! You will never regret starting your business with this tool. Your success with your business depends on your connecting with people. The larger your warm list, the better your chances for success.

Now, let's tackle some things head on. There are many things that pop up in people's minds when they are asked to connect with their warm market to build their business. Want us to take a stab at what might be in your head?

There is just no way I can come up with that many people on my list.

You won't know until you do it, now will you?

I don't want to call my friends until after I'm making money.

The solution is to watch your company Presentation again. Did it convince you that you can experience success? It will probably convince your friends, too, and they'll be glad you shared it with them. Don't you want them to know about it?

That person wouldn't possibly be interested in a home-based business.

Never, ever pre-judge people for this business because they could end up as a member in someone else's company. You ask - let them decide!

That person wouldn't possibly listen to me. I'm not important enough. They'll probably laugh at me!

You are the one holding an incredible business opportunity. Those people you think are so important are probably wishing they had a way out of their stress-filled lives. Isn't it more important that you think enough of them to show them your opportunity? Go ahead, make a "chicken list" - those people on your list you're scared to death to talk to. Tackle them one at a time.

Your Warm Market is crucially important to your creating Financial Freedom. Take it seriously. Okay, get to work on your list now!! Maybe you already made your list of 100 but now want to add more. Great!

> Sitting still and wishing makes no person great. The good Lord sends the fishing, but you must dig the bait!

The steel worker paused for a moment to wipe his brow. Sweat from a solid day's work never bothered him. He knew his son benefitted from the private schools he attended. His wife cleaned houses and worked as hard, or harder, than he did. Working extra and working harder proved to be an answer to the financial crunch he felt when he paid bills. In the rare times he saw Keith, his son never forget to tell him *thank you* for working so hard.

He would zoom in from school, blue eyes ablaze, brown hair a mess, scattering joy with every step. Stopping long enough to recount tidbits about his day, he enjoyed life immensely. Seeing that joy in his son's face, made these long double shifts worth every second. He proudly worked for his son's future. He and his wife believed in Keith and wanted more for him. He knew Keith truly understood they worked for his benefit. He always saw the emotion of gratitude deeply at work in his son.

Keith Ferrazzi grew up in Pittsburgh to working class parents and attended both Yale as an undergraduate and Harvard Business School for his graduate degree. His humble background fostered many attributes, but the overwhelming sense of *gratitude* toward his parents influenced him most. *"Generosity in relationships is the cornerstone of success"* is more than a "Keithism." It is a foundational principal for *all* of his life.

Ferrazzi Greenlight is a highly successful sales and marketing consulting firm based out of Los Angeles, California. Before creating his firm, Keith held success by its tail. He is the youngest ever Chief Marketing Officer of a Fortune 500 company, a Chief Executive Officer for an "interactive entertainment consultancy," and a New York Times bestselling author.

Ferrazzi Greenlight's motto is, *relationships: make connections, expand frontiers, create breakthroughs, foster understanding.*

His public speaking motto is, *"your success and joy powered by relationships."*

Yet Keith's answer to how he achieved such overwhelming success (he has been called the "most connected man" in the world) may surprise you. *"Our job is to step back and figure out ways to help others reach their* goals...their real dreams and aspirations. You have to take the risk and be vulnerable first... With the right approach, in five minutes you can develop a level of intimacy with somebody you've never met before that is deeper than what you probably have with people who share cubicles and office space within a rope's throw of you."

Keith takes his "connections" very seriously. In 2005, he established *Big Task Weekend,* a multi media event where high corporate executives with companies like KRAFT, Safeway, Del Monte, Kaiser, WebMD, and AARP collaborate with *each other* to influence and affect the communities *and the world* in which they operate.

These executives honestly evaluate and creatively act upon the problems people face. The sometimes "in your face" presentations leave no doubt that corporations face social responsibilities that extend beyond the office door. In fact, the thought is - the larger the shareholder base, the larger their responsibility. These weekends (which are by invitation only) include the biggest names from the largest and most widespread businesses in America. Officers from diverse companies, who would not normally network, now have lasting relationships.

"Big Task is a fusion of informative panels, presentations full of shock and awe, and life-enhancing personal development opportunities. The new connections that are forged become long lasting, meaningful and tap-able relationships providing resources that can be accessed as members move through implementation of actions."

Honesty, integrity, and accountability are paramount in building intimate trust, whether it is in personal or business relationships.WOW! Can you learn something from Keith? Sounds like good solid advice. Keith seems to have found what our parents and grandparents tried to teach us. Treat people well, play nice, and be friends! And you will succeed. Keith certainly did!

Today as you work on your life, remember that building relationships just may be the key you are missing as you build your business. Remember Keith as you reach out to others. Practice being grateful for those around you, and look for ways to connect!

21) Use Safelists (particularly credit-based safelists) to promote BIZ OP in a no-cost or low-cost way. (Just do a Google search on Safelists.)

Date, Action & Results

_____

_____

_____

_____

_____

> "The one major thing I do is that I belong to a lot of forums and I advertise my Biz Op in my signature with the link to my website. I also do this with all my emails."

22) Send out emails to everyone in your email address book. Invite them to look at, and join, your Biz Op. Provide them with a link to your business site. Send out multiple emails with the same subject line spaced a few days apart. Then use the same email body but change the subject line.

Date, Action & Results

_____

_____

_____

_____

_____

23) Leave your business cards or invitation cards at the restaurant with the tip. If you're going to leave a lousy tip you might not want to do this. :) Leave a great tip, and they're much more likely to take a look!

Date, Action & Results

_____

_____

_____

_____

_____

24) Keep a daily list of your activities. Use a small spiral notebook and keep track of what you're doing. Refer to it often to make sure you're not repeating something that you've tried before that didn't work. "Activity Counts" but make sure it's activity that is moving your business forward, not just busy work.

Date, Action & Results

_____

_____

_____

_____

_____

_____

POWER MODULE # 6

What If You Don't Know Anyone?

We've talked a lot about making your warm market list, then contacting all those people. But let's face reality here. You might be one of those people who just moved into town yesterday, after living for 20 years in the African Bush. Or you might have been in so many home-based businesses that anyone you know runs when they see you coming. You've thought about buying leads of people wanting a business, but you really don't have the money. NO PROBLEM – as long as you're willing to do the things it will take to be a success!

I'm already teaching you how to build on the Internet if you have no money. But if you're totally committed to doing whatever it takes to succeed, I'm about to tell you what you need to know to build your business with the people around you – whether you know them or not!

This letter is going to concentrate on what you do if your warm market is fairly non-existent. Don't be discouraged if that is the case for you. One of my friends, Stuart, learned a valuable lesson years ago when he started with his company. The truth it holds is very powerful. Stuart had just moved into a new town. He didn't know anyone, except his brother – the one who had introduced him to his new company. Things didn't look very promising but he was determined to make it work. Here's what he did...

One day his brother threw him the keys to his Mercedes and said, *"Go find people for me to talk to. Just get them to a meeting."* Stuart took the car and started driving around. He was in a panic, his thoughts racing; *How do you meet people? What do you do? How do you meet people? What do you do?*

Hours later, covered with sweat in a well air-conditioned Mercedes, he was no closer to an answer. He looked down at the gas tank, realized he was near empty, and then realized he had no idea where to get diesel fuel. At the first stop light he rolled his window down and asked the person in the car next to him. *"Are you from around here?"* Then he proceeded to ask for directions to a gas station that sold diesel.

He drove off, his thoughts still racing – *How do you meet people? What do you do? How do you meet people? What do you...* He stopped in mid-thought, realizing he had just indeed met someone! Now he was eager to get to the gas station.

Stuart jumped out of his car, started pumping gas, and then turned to the man behind him. He knew what to do. *"Hey, are you from around here?"*

"Yeah," the man responded. *"Where do you want to go?"*

Whoops! He hadn't thought far enough head for that question. Thankfully he was able to think fast. *"Oh, no, I don't need to go anywhere. I just had a question. I've got a company that is exploding all over the country, and I'm looking for people who want to earn some extra income from home. Do you know anyone like that?"*

"Yeah. Me. What is it?"

Oh no! Another question he wasn't ready for! More fast thinking... *"Look, I don't have time to talk about it right now. Let me get your phone number. I'll give you a call."* He got his number and drove off.

He'd found his answer! Over the next week he spent 8 hours a day asking people, *"Hey, are you from around here?"* The next week, 18 of those people showed up at his brother's meeting. 6 months later he had by-passed everyone else in his brother's organization! How? He spent 8 hours a day asking that question!

You can do the same thing! Maybe you don't have meetings. No problem. Send them to your website. Get their name, email address and phone number. Send them an email with your name in the subject line or something about meeting them that day. You've got a great prospect!

It really is just a numbers game. If you talk to enough people, you will build an incredible business.

So here we are. You have your list. You know how to talk to your warm market. You know how to approach your cold market. The rest is up to you. **YOU SIMPLY HAVE TO GO DO IT!!**

POWER STORY # 6

Leanna, at age 9, had what she considered an exquisite idea. *"Mom, everyone comments on my hair! Every time I use Great Grandma's pomade, strangers stop and compliment me. It's good stuff. We should sell this!"*

"Honey, we don't know anything about running a business and we don't have time. Maybe when you're older," came the understandable parental reply.

Two years later at age 11, Leanna came back to her parents armed with ammunition: information about small business ownership; obtaining a tax i.d. number; and lists of potential customers requesting more products from a few samples she'd supplied. She even had a name, *Leanna's!*

I can only imagine the dinner conversation at their house. It wouldn't have been your typical teen drama routine over meatloaf, salad, and potatoes.

"Leanna, have you finished pulling orders for tomorrow?

"Yes, Mom, they are completely ready!"

"Dad, do you have the invoices ready?"

"Yes dear. Honey, did you call Great Grandma and ask her to increase the order for the facial scrub with lavender and the mango-tropical Shea lotion? Those orders last week nearly depleted our inventory and we're getting in more every day."

"Talked to her today and everything is ready. Leanne and I will pick them up after school tomorrow."

Now, in 2008, *at age 13*, Leanna is CEO of Leanna's, INC, with eight employees, and pulls in $100,000 yearly from her hair and body care business!

As an *eighth grader*, she studies by day and directs operations of her multi-level business at night.

As an accomplished motivational speaker, Leanna has enjoyed a feature in Ebony magazine, and been interviewed on Sally Jesse's radio talk show.

She's been featured by the New York News Day Reporter, and numerous radio stations, newspapers, and magazines, as well as been a featured guest speaker around New York State.

She's even expanded from hair care products to a designing a teen magazine called *Thriving Thirteen* (see ThrivingThirteen.com) which is *"written by preteens for preteens and their parents."* She has a kid's representative program where youngsters, with help from their parents, can sell Leanna's products, gaining not only financial benefits but also invaluable life skills. She isn't just making money; she regularly contributes to at least three different charitable organizations.

As #12 of the top *30 under 30 successful entrepreneurs* in the U.S., Leanna understands the responsibilities of making money and doing her own thing.

She has a wonderful positive and upbeat message. *"My success is the reason that I reached out to kids all over America. I travel the country giving speeches to motivate kids and young adults."*

Wow! Wonder if I could clone her attitude for myself! It's amazing for a young woman of any age, much less one that is just now a teenager!

I know we can learn from Leanna. She is doing her research and expanding her product line as interest grows. She is giving back to the communities that support her by encouraging other people - kids and adults, to look for ways to give their all!

"I will always tell them to believe in themselves no matter how young they are. I tell them to research ideas they may have and not be afraid to ask questions. It does not work out the first time, my signature phrase to them is: when you fall, pick yourself up, dust yourself off and keep going. Learning is ongoing. I've learned that I must remain determined and tenacious. I must continue to have structure and discipline."

Today as you go out, live, breathe, and love, let's remember the beautiful inspiration from Leanna: *"Believe in ourselves, ask questions and keep going!"*

25) Use your personal email address as your business address for your Biz Op so you have a better chance of getting through spam filters. There's no doubt who the email is from. Address the person by name whenever possible, and include their name in the Subject Line as well. Include a full signature-brief autobiography plus your phone number at the bottom of each email.

Date, Action & Results

26) Invite 4 or 5 friends or family members over for coffee or tea. Introduce your Biz Op by having them watch a video. Have your computer available and an Internet connection so people can sign up right then and there. Have light refreshments and provide a free gift. Be sure to have information (flyers, Invitation Cards, etc.) for people to take home if they aren't ready to sign-up. Make sure you get everyone's email address who comes to your informal get together.

Do NOT hide the purpose of the get together or they will feel deceived. It's best to tell them you want to share an exciting business opportunity and have few people come, then it is to have a lot of people come who never want to be your friends again! Honesty is always best.

Date, Action & Results

_____

_____

_____

_____

_____

_____

27) Use your favorite search engine to find free leads. Here are a few: listbandit.com, sysm.com, simplerleads.com, tripleyourlist.com. A word of caution: not all "free" sites are really free. Sometimes the only thing that is free is the actual signing up and everything else requires payment. You'll just have to do some searching because things change so fast.

Date, Action & Results

_____

_____

_____

_____

_____

_____

_____

_____

_____

28) Take advantage of the free networks online. One such network is SaleSpider.com and is so huge it won't matter how many Biz Op people use it. It is free to sign up and you can add your Biz Op to any network. You can also place free classified ads.

Date, Action & Results

_____

_____

_____

_____

_____

_____

_____

Lost – somewhere between sunrise and sunset – one golden hour encrusted with sixty silver minutes, each studded with sixty diamond seconds. No reward is offered. They are lost and gone forever.

Who Will Win The Biggest?

Let's start with a very basic truth... ***The person who contacts the most people will be the biggest winner. Let's repeat that for you...*** The person who contacts the most people will be the biggest winner. One more time just to make sure you got it...

> ### THE PERSON WHO CONTACTS THE MOST PEOPLE WILL BE THE BIGGEST WINNER!!

Now, I want to address a very important issue. Not everyone wants to be a big winner. You only want to add a few people on your frontline? You just want to make enough additional income to get by? That's great! It's your business. You can do with it whatever you want. Get your people on your frontline. Make sure they are great people and then help them duplicate. In time, you will see your income grow.

But what if you want more? What if you aren't content with being average? What if you want to make big money? What if you want to have a huge frontline in order to maximize your income? Then you'll need to pay close attention to this information. And you'll have to determine that you are going to work the numbers.

That's really what it is all about. ***We've said it a hundred times already; building a successful home-based business (no matter what company you're with) is a numbers game.*** It's really very simple. Some people you talk to are going to say yes. Some are going to say no. You simply have to talk to enough people – to make sure enough say yes – to make sure your business grows as large as you want it to.

At the beginning you are going to have to talk to more people because you're learning how to present your business. You're learning how to handle questions and objections. You're learning how to be the kind of confident leader people want to follow. It will take talking to more people to get the yeses you want to get.

How many people do you need to talk to? That depends on your dreams and goals, but let's look at one scenario. Let's assume you are working your business on a part-time basis. (That is going to be true for the majority of your team in the beginning.) Let's also assume that when you make a commitment, you keep it. The commitment you've made is to contact at least **2** new people a day.

To be honest, that should be the minimum commitment you make toward building your business if you really are serious about making it grow. Go back and look at all the ideas for connecting with people. It's not such a big deal. Whether that is your warm market; people you meet around town; or people you are calling on the phone – they are people you actually TALK to. We're not talking about people who don't answer the phone; or people you just think about talking to. These are people you have spoken to and then sent an email to; people you have invited to a meeting; people you have directed to your website with a personal Invitation or flyer; or people you have spoken with and sent to your website.

If you're working exclusively on the Internet (something I don't recommend, but know some people will choose to do), you'll need to contact many more, but then it will be so much easier. You will want to increase your number to 15-20 a day. But let's assume you're incorporating actual human contact…

Okay, I think you know what I mean by 2 people a day. Let's assume you are going to do this 6 days a week, which means you will have contacted 12 people a week – or 50 people a month. See how the numbers are adding up? Now, what can you expect from these numbers? Every scenario will be different, but on an average you can expect to sign up one out of every 5 personal contacts, and 1 out of every 20 Internet contacts. Not too good, you say? Let's keep Inspecting the numbers. (And keep in mind, your averages might be lower while you're building your skills and learning your business – give yourself time to learn!)

Now, let's look at those numbers. You've signed up 10 members on your front line in your first month! If even half of your team is duplicating that, you've now got close to 60 in your team. More importantly, you've already positioned yourself for amazing income!

You maintain your commitment of 2 people a day – making sure you also work with your existing team members as a great sponsor. My guess is that as you see your business growing you're going to talk to more, but let's just stick with your commitment. 2 people a day. 12 a week. 50 a month (4.5 weeks a month). 10 new members a month. Where does that take us in one year? 600 contacts a year. 120 new members in your first year. It will become easier and easier as you go because your new prospects will be blown away by how fast your team is growing.

And that's only your first year. You're probably full time by now and talking to tons of people, or simply hanging out on a beach somewhere, but our scenario is for a commitment of 2, and I want you to see how small numbers can add up. Your second year you do the same thing and add another 120 people to your frontline. What will *that* do to your entire team? Wow!

So here is the moral of this story. Decide on your commitment. Then do it! Work the numbers. Make the numbers work for you. Be consistently consistent. **There is no secret to success in a home-based business.** It really IS a simple matter of numbers. Now, repeat after me...

THE PERSON WHO CONTACTS THE MOST PEOPLE WILL BE THE BIGGEST WINNER!!

Got It??

The cardiac monitor beeps and Libby moves nearer. The baby needs more oxygen. Its thin chest walls are heaving to keep the airflow constant. As a pediatric cardiovascular intensive care nurse, Libby loves her patients and her job. The kids coming in for care deal with their heart problems with the expertise of someone eons older. Libby provides care and devotion to her little ones...paying strict attention to both them and the details of their care. Libby's flyaway red hair, compassionate eyes and quick beautiful smile radiate joy in the hospital's ICU room.

As her work is over for the week, Libby shifts her mind to the tasks of the coming weekend.

Libby is a competent, experienced rock-climber and slackliner. A slackliner is someone who balance walks across a thin line stretched across two points. Slacklining is a sport where the line stretches and bounces – like a very thin, flat, long trampoline. Slackliners walk just ten feet off the ground.

As comfortable as Libby is with slacklining, highlining was something she had never done.

Libby has friends who are highliners who combine high elevation with the balance sport of slacklining. After securing the line high between two points, a highliner walks barefoot across the line with only a simple rescue harness hundreds and even thousands of feet above ground. A highliner walks from one end to the other, and hopefully doesn't fall. The point of highlining is simply to cross from one side to the other. The "anchor points" can be buildings or mountains, and usually span several yards.

The adrenaline rush and sense of accomplishment when a highliner makes a successful crossing is overwhelming. Facing fear and increasing self-confidence are two by-products of such attempts.

"I can do that," Libby thought, as she listened to her friends' wondrous stories of their experiences with thin air and eagle-like vantage points. A yearning stirred within her spirit.

Her thoughts raced skyward. *"I want to move to the next level,"* she thought to herself.

Excited as her yearning became much more than just a desire, she heard herself say to her friends, *"I'm gonna do it. I'm gonna highline. I want to try. I want to feel the wind blow my breath away. I want to step across into the unknown. I know my limit with slacklining...but I don't know what it feels like at 1000 feet or even 2000 feet above the earth! I'll never know if I don't try. I can't do it alone. I can't wait! Will you help me?"*

Libby teamed up with experienced highliners and chose Lost Arrow Spire Highline in Yosemite National Park. Considered by all highliners as a "mecca" for the sport, the last *successful* crossing was over 20 years ago - by a man. Others attempted to cross Lost Arrow but very, very few succeed. In addition, *no woman had **ever** done it!*

Now, you've got to get the picture. The height of Lost Arrow Spire is equal to TWO Empire State buildings stacked on top of each other, plus another 400 feet! Her distance above the earth would be a whopping 2,890 feet! The only things between her and the tree-studded ground would be nearly 3,000 feet of thin air, a highline, and her safety harness!

Do you think she got it on the first try? Nope!

Libby tried *several* times. She kept falling as she fought to keep her balance. Her climbing buddies encouraged her every step of the way. She would fall, dangle precariously from the highline with her legs wrapped around it (think of a sloth in an upside down position), and then haul herself to the starting side to begin again. Each fall was captured on video, so the viewer would know it took ***her more than one time to get it right!***

Even though Libby fell more than once, **she never quit**. Even though more experienced highliners were on her team, they feared such an extreme height.

But Libby didn't!

She learned from her falls and mistakes. She listened to her team's advice. She put into practice those things she had learned from rock climbing and slacklining. Mostly she kept her eyes focused straight ahead...always thinking about the next step.

Left, right, left, right...one foot in front of the other as the mountain wind teased her hair.

Finally, with arms outstretched and her hair bandana blown away, Libby realized she had one last step to go! She had made it! She had done it! With a graceful and grateful last step, she hopped atop a narrow rock formation nearly 3,000 feet above the ground and celebrated her crossing!

She had done what no woman had ever done and few men would ever do! She had successfully maneuvered her longest line walk ever - over 55 feet long - and of course we know it was one of the highest line walks ever!

I think it's interesting to note that the same skill works at 10 feet off the ground as it does at 3,000! The same advice works no matter the altitude. That is wisdom for those of us who have our feet on the ground!

Just keep putting one foot in front of the other. Keep making attempts when you fail and fall.

I watched a video of Libby's walk and while the focus is on her, you see and hear her team of encouragers. They call out to her, laugh with her, help her, and celebrate with her! They are as excited as she is! They accompanied her on the 3,000-foot climb and sit exposed on mere inches of a mountain ledge. Together, they had dreamed and worked for this day

I think that is the wonder of Libby's story. Together, a team of folks dreamed she could do the walk, and then they set out together to document the process. The team stayed with her until the end, braving many of the same elements as she did as they shared this awesome experience.

You know, you too have a team of folks that dream with you. They believe in your progress and your steps. Tap into the power of that on a daily basis and your business will explode!

29) Never underestimate your signature line. It is a very powerful tool. Use it in all your email messages including a banner or a link to your Biz Op website. If you belong to forums and they allow it, make sure to put your BIZ OP website in your signature. Consider putting something like this in your signature (or as a P.S.): A Special Fr.ee Gift Just For You (then add your domain name or BIZ OP business site URL) Use sentences like "The 1st Online Business 100% Free" (or whatever works for your Business) under your name. People will ask about it which makes it very easy to talk about your BIZ OP. Put lots of information about yourself in your signature. Let people know you are a real person.

Date, Action & Results

_____

_____

_____

_____

_____

30) Make a flyer (preferably in color is possible) with tear-off tags at the bottom that have your domain URL on them. Put them up on laundry bulletin boards and other public places (get permission first). Check back periodically to replenish or replace the flyer.

Date, Action & Results (put a copy of your flyer right here!)

_____

_____

_____

_____

31) Go to a public place with a Wi-Fi (wireless) connection so you can SHOW people the BIZ OP opportunity when you get a chance over a conversation. Yeah – you'll have to have your laptop! ☺

Date, Action & Results

_____

_____

_____

_____

_____

32) Look for sites that offer FREE online classified ads. A great site is classifiedsforfree.com because once you have your original ad in place (takes about 30-40 minutes to place it in all the countries, U.S. states and U.S. cities), you can renew it in a matter of 5 minutes. It is the least time consuming free classified website I have found.) If you are posting ads, you'll need to track them since you'll be posting in lots of sites.

Date, Action & Results

_____

_____

_____

_____

_____

_____

_____

POWER MODULE # 8

How To Attract The Right People

What kind of people do you want on your Biz Op team? Don't you want to attract the right type of people that will help you build a great organization? Of course you do. The question is – how do you do it?

The truth is, we attract to our reality who we are and what we become. You're convinced you have a great Biz Op. You are working to become a better person. You also have to focus on attracting the right quality people. You simply can't build a successful business without people. This is not something you can do yourself. Duplication is absolutely necessary, so you might as well learn how to do it right from the beginning. Attracting and choosing the right people is paramount to your success.

The best way for you to attract the right people is to become the right person. **Become a great person first – the rest will find you.** Don't read this and skip merrily on. Go back and read it a few times. Here, we will repeat it for you. **Become a great person first – the rest will find you.** One more time. **Become a great person first – the rest will find you.**

This won't be an overnight process. It will take time to become a better person. As you become a better person, you will attract better people and better situations to your reality. There is no "I" in the word TEAM.

Spend time developing yourself as a person. Develop your character. Your charisma. Your leadership skills. Your confidence level. Your work ethics. Your strong caring for those around you. Develop your knowledge. As you develop into a better person, the better people you are looking for will come to you. Sound like a lot of work? It is. But what else will give you the kind of payoff this will? And we're not just talking about money. Won't every area of your life be more rewarding and fulfilling if you are becoming a better person? You bet it will!

You will not become successful alone. You HAVE to attract the right people who you can assist in reaching their goals in order for you to reach your own goals. Some of your greatest rewards will come from watching those around you succeed beyond their wildest dreams.

Read books. Listen to tapes. Go to seminars. Critique yourself honestly, then be willing to work on your faults and weaknesses. You must learn to heal yourself before you can heal others. You must learn to love yourself before you can learn to love others. You might be saying, *"Wait a minute. I thought I was just building a business to make money."*

Let's clear that up now. **Wrong!** You are building a PEOPLE business. It's all about people. The kind of person you are. The kind of people you work with. The kind of people you want to work with. Your greatest reward will not be the money you make. It will be the person you become. It will be the people who enrich your life. Be willing to pay the price to make this true.

Are you paralyzed by fear? Are you hampered by low self-esteem? Are you shy? Be willing to take the steps to conquer these areas. Surround yourself with people who can help you get where you want to be.

Let's go a little deeper here. What do you believe your reality to be? Where have you come from? A bad marriage? A bad family? Years of abuse? Abandonment? Being made to feel like a lousy person? Have one of these things become your reality? You are going to bring it into your business. You are going to continue to attract bad people and bad situations into your reality. Remember, this is a people business. This reality is what you will attract to yourself.

We attract who we are. The bright side is that we can also attract who we become. What are you becoming? If money weren't an issue what would you be doing with your time? Become an exceptional person. Do something exceptional with your life. Attract exceptional people.

FEAR keeps you from approaching other people. Unfortunately, it's your own attitude and beliefs that make your reality. There are people who will say, *"No one wants to do this business." "I can't find anyone who will sign up." "I can't even get a simple yes." "I just can't make this business work for me."* They are speaking their reality.

Then they start to change. They become better people. Then the people they contact change. **Not really** – but since your own reality has changed, so do the people you contact. Suddenly they want to join your Biz Op. They are the leaders you are looking for. If you believe you are going to attract leaders to your team – you will. If you can manage to get hold of the truth that your beliefs become your reality you will win with your Biz Op. You will win in the game of life. Study this concept until you realize its truth. Successful people all through the ages realize the truth of the power of their thoughts to transform their lives. Join them in realizing that truth and your life will change.

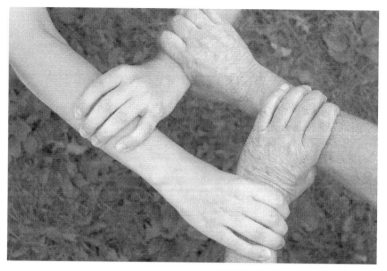

So, who are you attracting to yourself? I do not pretend to know the reality of your life. I don't know where you come from. I don't know what life lessons the Universe has for you to learn. I don't know if you have given, given, given in other areas and now your time in your Biz Op is your chance to harvest all you have given by your building an explosive business right from the beginning. I don't know if you have a charismatic personality that draws people to you no matter what you're doing. Likewise, I don't know if the Universe wants to teach you the lessons of persistence and refusing to give up - making you work harder for your success in your Biz Op. I don't know if you're innately shy and will have to work hard to overcome that before you can succeed. Only YOU can know the answers to those questions.

Tell yourself every day – I ATTRACT WINNERS TO MY TEAM. Say it over and over. Out loud - over and over. Repeat it to yourself, over and over. Keep saying it to yourself until you believe it – until it becomes your reality. When you truly believe it – it WILL become your reality. Don't just read this. **DO IT!**

> Coming together is a beginning.
> Keeping together is progress.
> Working together is success.
>
> ~ Henry Ford

POWER STORY # 8

Three pink slips. Three layoffs. Three dreams lying in the corner. Brothers Justin and Jef Sewell, and friend Larry Kersten, sat in the office with hearts on the floor. Each was a highly trained professional. Kersten even held a Ph.D in Organizational Development. Each had worked (past tense) for the same prestigious firm. Since a recent restructuring brought in a board of engineers, and these three were not engineers, each was now without a job!

They could become country western balladeers crooning out: *"Blue despair and agony on me. Deep dark depression, excessive misery. If it weren't for bad luck we'd have no luck at all, blue despair and agony on me."*

Instead of singing, one of the crew picked up a sleek four-color magazine brimming with motivational posters, cups, calendars, cards, mouse pads, and t-shirts that screamed rejection at the men. These products originally

 designed to *"brighten your cubicle with positive affirmation"* taunted them. Teasing the group, the products seemed to mock their dilemma.

Rejection dripped from their pores as their dignity withered. Visions of homelessness began taking shape on their collective horizons. Then one of them picked up that motivational mayhem of a magazine and deliberately misquoted the words on a poster.

Holding up the magazine and with tongue in check, he quipped: *"If at first you don't succeed, failure may be your style. ©"*

The original poster set a beautiful scene with the well worn cliché..."if at first you don't succeed try, try again."

The group chuckled.

Again they parodied a positive quote. Then again with the slightest amount of sarcasm oozing into their creative words, an idea formed. An idea whose foundation lay at the base reality of the professional world from which they had just gotten the boot.

They would form a new company based on the truth. The truth behind companies who promise one thing yet deliver the contrary. The real emotions a person experiences when a board member shakes your hand and stabs your back - simultaneously.

The name of their new company: dispair.com :-(™

That is exactly what Justin, Jef, and CEO Larry Kersten have triumphantly accomplished.

From that grey day in 1988 to today's multimillion dollar enterprise, these men have laughed their way into our offices and meetings, and onto our screensavers, backs, hands, and walls with their satirical misrepresentations of business life. They took their layoff to heart, but successfully turned it all the way around. They didn't lose heart – they gained success!

What is their take on such themes as procrastination, teamwork and achievement? Read below to get a taste of what despair.com :-(has to say!

 "**Procrastination:** *Hard work often pays off after time, but laziness always pays off now. ©*"

"**Teamwork** - *A few harmless flakes working together can unleash an avalanche of destruction. ©*"

"**Achievement** - *You can do anything you set your mind to when you have vision, determination, and an endless supply of expendable labor. ©*"

Life is hard but these guys found a rich nugget in making light of that hardness.

Millions of people worldwide read their blog, subscribe to their Twitter feed, and order dollars upon dollars worth of merchandise. Their lighthearted outlook hits many humorous notes of reality and relief. With millions in the bank, they abundantly enjoy helping people laugh at their own despair!

Today, as you go about accomplishing the many tasks on your "to do list," look for the lighter side of life. Go for your dreams in any direction you can. Even if that means making the proverbial lemonade out of life's lemons! You'll be so glad you did!

33) Go through all the business cards you've collected over the years and call, write or email them. Entrepreneurs are usually open for additional streams of income.

Date, Action & Results

_____

_____

_____

_____

_____

34) Advertise your Biz Op all over the Internet. Type FREE STUFF, FREE ADVERTISEMENTS, FREE SITES, etc. in your favorite search engine.

Date, Action & Results

_____

_____

_____

_____

_____

_____

_____

_____

35) Use the Coop Promotion type of approach. Everyone can work a business regardless of their background, ideas or beliefs. Believe in teamwork and open the doors of your Biz Op to all. Communicate, share and work together as a team. Treat each new member as an independent franchise owner.

Date, Action & Results

_____

_____

_____

_____

_____

_____

_____

36) Anytime someone hands you something - a note, flyer, change for a small purchase like an ice cream cone – exchange whatever it is they are handing you with your business card or invitation card.

Date, Action & Results

_____

_____

_____

_____

37) Permission email is a great way to share your Biz Op. Basically with permission emails you do a search for classified advertising through a search engine. Go to that classified site and start reading through the ads. Hit the reply button and simply ask for the advertiser's permission to send your information to them. Here's an example:

Hello _____,

I saw your ad for _____ on (classified site name). I'll check out yours if you'll check out mine. ☺ May I please send you some more information?

Your name

Date, Action & Results (Write Your Own)

_____

_____

_____

_____

_____

_____

_____

_____

_____

_____

_____

_____

_____

POWER MODULE # 9

Why A Home-Based Business?

Let's talk about this incredible industry you have involved yourself in – Home-Based Businesses. Let's face it. Over the years there have been companies that have given Home-Based Businesses a bad name, but the concept is sound and has carried many people to financial freedom – if they took consistent, positive action.

1) A home-based business has, quite literally, no downside risk. You see, most businesses require significant capital before you can even hang up a sign. I imagine you have started your business for less than $1000 – many for much less. Amazing!

2) There is literally no ceiling, no limit on earnings. A lawyer can only bill for so many hours in the day and a doctor can only perform a handful of surgeries a day. Some great people working in traditional businesses haven't had a raise in 10 years. But, in your case, you can create a raise for your family every day if you choose. As you build your business you will be paid on dozens, then hundreds, and then thousands of individuals. Truly, the only limit on your business is what you put there yourself. It doesn't matter what your sex, race, marital status, income level, or educational level is. It doesn't matter if you are home-bound in a wheelchair. It doesn't matter if you've never succeeded at anything before. What you do with your business is completely up to you. How much money you make is completely up to you!

3) Time freedom is directly commensurate with wealth and prosperity. In our opinion, nothing in life equals the joy of spending quality time doing the things we most enjoy with the people we most love. In traditional professions, small businesses, sales or corporate management, everyone is struggling through 60-80 hour work weeks to have, maybe, a Sunday afternoon with their family. Nothing is more precious than free time, and those of us who have achieved it are excited about an opportunity that offers this precious commodity to others.

4) There need not be any stress at all in your business. Do you know that the number one trend in America is stress-induced coronary? It's no longer just a risk for men; it's also an increasing risk for women. With your own home-based business, if you aren't having fun, you aren't doing it right. You're making new friends; you're building great relationships; you're building financial security for the rest of your life! Have fun!!

5) You get to invest in the Home-Based Business Plan. What do we mean? Well, most people out there have decided to invest in the Forty Year Plan. That's the best folks can hope for in traditional business. By age 25, most people have an idea of what kind of work they want to do; how they want to make money in their lives. They work hard at whatever it is they decide to do. But 40 years later, out of a typical 100 people; 5 are still working, 36 are dead, 54 are dead broke (or at least earning far less than when they were employed), 4 are well off, and 1 person is wealthy. Thus, the 40 year plan means that for 4 decades most of us go back and forth from home to work, back and forth, back and forth, like a caged lion... and yet at the end of that time only 5 out of 100 have something to show for it! Yikes!

In stark contrast is the Home-Based Business Plan. Work diligently to build your team. It could take a few months or a few years. It all depends on you. Build a residual income based on the power of your company and you're set for life.

6) It is said that "Recognition is our most sought after reward in life. Babies cry for it and grown men die for it." Everyone loves recognition. It's true for us. We bet it's true for you, too. The rewards of helping people change their lives with a home-based business go far beyond money made. There is nothing quite like people thanking you for introducing them to a business that has given them the freedom they dreamed of for so long!

7) You are truly in the right place at the right time. People all over the world are searching for a way to create financial freedom. You have the answer for them. All you have to do is follow everything in this book and you'll create the life of your dreams!

Open the door to my friend Suess' home, and usually the smell of lavender wafts over you. A double wicked lavender jar candle burns nearly continuously whenever she is at home. Dinner at her house includes anywhere from one to nine candles on the tabletop.

She has trained her family and friends. Stop for a visit and she'll train you too!!

You'll be instructed to stop and smell their fragrance, stop and watch the flame dance with color, and stop to enjoy a meal made more delicious by the candlelight's graceful dance. There is no more relaxing atmosphere than one enhanced by the sight and smell of candles.

Yet, there are two women in Mississippi whose candles have created even more than a pleasant home. Their candles provide a highly successful business endeavor. But candles were not the first line of work this mother/daughter duo shared.

You know, it is fairly common to have a registered nurse for a mother. However, it is uncommon to go to college simultaneously with her! Becky waited until her girls were older to pursue her lifetime dream of nursing. She was so much older in fact, that she attended college with her daughters!

Becky was deeply satisfied with her beloved nursing profession, while Kim enjoyed a career as a medical lab technician.

Working professionally filled many needs. Keeping her home bright and welcoming fulfilled other needs as well. Candles lit a warm glow in Becky's heart. In addition, learning to actually make those candles satisfied her diverse creativity needs. Weekends and free evenings were spent learning to pour molds and create these molten beauties. Word of mouth advertising with one small retail store seemed sufficient. Soon however the quality of their product resulted in dramatically increased orders. Along with her daughter, Becky soon found herself co-proprietor of an exploding candle business while still pursuing a hectic nursing career.

As one success in the candle industry led to another, Becky and Kim struggled to find time *to live.* Soon their weekend hobby lit such a bright flame of success that their lives could not contain both professions. First one, and then the other quit the medical field and devoted her full energy to candles. The move has paid off tremendously.

Flash forward a few years and in 2008, their company *Wicks N More* employs 60 workers in an 83,000 square foot building. Their products are now available in some 3,000 stores across the USA. Their company *"is the leading manufacturer of exquisite, hand-poured, decorative scented candles.*

Manufacturing candles all day long, mother and daughter may not agree on every candle's name or color but they do agree on one thing. *"From day one, we had the same expectations and goal. We are always focusing on having a better candle and putting out a high-quality product."*

Today, as you work out the differences in your life, I hope you are pursuing your dreams with your whole heart. Put yourself out there and let the world know your dreams are coming.

Don't hide them where no one can see. I know that even as Becky and Kim struggled at first to balance their careers, it was only through that struggle that their true passions shone. Like their candles and their success, I know they would say it is worth every step they took to get where they are today.

I hope you realize that today can be a new beginning for you. Take some positive steps and soon you'll see your dreams coming true. It is a process but you've got to get started!

38) When searching the Internet for places to put free ads, be sure to use different search engines. Each one can pull up different results. Now you have even more places to place your ad!

Date, Action & Results

_____

_____

_____

_____

_____

_____

39) Use catchy phrases on flyers to draw attention: Work From Home, Need Additional Income, Apprentice Wanted, $$$ Earn Additional $$$. Test different ones to see what gets the best response.

Date, Action & Results

_____

_____

_____

_____

_____

_____

40) When inviting someone to look at BIZ OP, you can use wording like this: "One of my greatest joys is to share my Biz Op with people because it helps so many people. I hope you will accept my gift to you." Then give your domain name or BIZ OP business site URL. *If your Biz Op is a good one, it really is a GIFT to people!*

Date, Action & Results

_____

_____

_____

_____

_____

_____

41) If you are a member of a social networking site, be sure to welcome newcomers as soon as you see them. Get your link out there first. There are still lots of such groups without BIZ OP members.

Date, Action & Results

_____

_____

_____

_____

_____

_____

POWER MODULE # 10

Feel The Fear And DO It Anyway!

Some of you may experience the feeling of dread or fear when faced with approaching people about your Business Opportunity. Let's face it – it can be scary at times! People's reactions to your new business can deflate your attitude and sap your business-building energy -- but only if you let them!

No matter what you have done, or not done, to this point in your life - changing that is as simple as making a decision. Notice I didn't say easy - but it is *simple*. You simply need to make a decision to live the rest of your life differently than you have lived the first part of it. I don't care if you're 13 or 103. As long as you're still breathing, I believe there is purpose for your being here and you can make the rest of your life fulfilling and exciting.

The same is true for your business. No matter what you've done, or not done, to this point, you can make a decision to create exactly what you dream of that made you start your business in the first place. All of us have dreams. All of us also have fears. I was talking with one of my neighbors recently after I went for a long swim in the lake with her 11 year old daughter. It was a beautiful afternoon so I settled down to bask in the sun and talk for a few minutes. She was talking about her job and I could tell she wasn't exactly thrilled with it so I decided to ask my favorite question. "If you could do anything, what would it be?"

Her eyes lit up as she described the store she would like to have. When she fell silent I asked her, "What keeps you from doing it?"

She looked down for a moment, then met my eyes. "Fear of failure," she said softly.

How many of us struggle with that? I know I do. I don't care what someone does, how much money they make or how successful they are – they had to (and probably still have to) battle through fears. Everyone is just human – with fears, and hopes, and dreams.

It's okay to be afraid. If we're honest, every single one of us will admit to feeling that at one time or another. It's what we do with that fear that will determine how we live our lives. One of my favorite sayings is, *Feel the Fear and do it ANYWAY!* As you build your business or live your life, you are going to run into many things that make you afraid. That's okay. Feel the fear. But then go and DO the things you are afraid of. The very act of doing it will make you less fearful - until you find yourself walking in more and more power.

Take some time and write down the things you are scared of doing with your business. What are the fears that stop you from taking action? What can you do TODAY to take action to conquer those fears? (I'm going to give you a lot of space to write these down because FEAR is the biggest reason most people fail in building a business. Have the courage to look it squarely in the face!

_____

_____

_____

_____

_____

_____

_____

_____

_____

_____

Caspian was a new addition to my household... he had shown up in the front yard of my 100 year old Virginia farmhouse one early morning. He looked like a Chocolate Labrador Retriever, but he was skin and bones, covered with ticks, fleas and sores, and had been shot – his skinny body riddled with buckshot. I took one look at this pathetic animal and told him he was home.

It took weeks of vet treatments, baths and many bowls of food, but he finally began to look like a dog that was going to make it. His bones began to disappear, his coat took on a shine, and he became my constant shadow to show his appreciation for me saving his life. He was always with me – except when I went upstairs to my office...

My home had a wide expanse of wooden stairs that led to the 2nd floor. Caspian was terrified of them. It didn't matter what I did to build his confidence, or what wonderful tidbit of food I tempted him with, he refused to climb those stairs. He would just cower at the bottom stair and shake all over whenever I got him near them. Yet when I went up to my office, he was overcome with despair at being separated from me, and laid at the bottom whimpering and whining.

I had no idea what had created this fear, and I had even less of an idea of how to conquer it. After two weeks of daily attempts, I finally gave up. If he didn't want to climb the stairs – so be it. But my only defense from his pitiful whining was to turn the music up any time I needed to be in my office. When I would leave my office and come downstairs, Caspian would erupt with frantic joy to be reunited once again.

About a month into this pattern, I was awakened one morning by a noise. I lay in bed trying to identify what it was.

Click, click, click... Silence. Click, click, click... Silence.

It kept on for close to fifteen minutes before my curiosity finally overwhelmed my desire to stay under the warm covers. I threw aside my quilt, grabbed a robe and went out to investigate. When I identified the source of the noise, I just stood there with my mouth wide open.

I watched as Caspian carefully climbed the stairs. *Click, click, click...* He got to the top, turned around, and then started back down. *Click, click, click...*

When he got to the bottom, he turned and gazed at me as if to say, *It's really no big deal. I can do this!*

And then he did it again, and again, and again... at least 25 more times – after already having done it for 15 minutes before I finally came to investigate.

I watched his confidence grow with each ascent and descent of the "dreaded stairs." His tongue hung out in joy and at the end his tail wagged his triumph over his fears. He knew he would never again have to be separated from me because of the stairs.

I already loved him, but that day I gained an incredible respect for his courage and resilience. I was also challenged about what I was willing to do to overcome *my* fears. *Was I willing to stare my fears in the face and then take the steps to overcome that fear? Was I willing to feel the fear, and then do it anyway? Was I willing to attack my fears, for as long as it took to overcome them?* I made a lot of decisions that day that have given me a much richer life – and I have Caspian to thank for it!

So now I pose the same questions to you: *Are you willing to stare your fears in the face and then take the steps to overcome them? Are you willing to feel the fear, and then do it anyway? Are you willing to attack your fears for as long as it takes to overcome them?*

Every time you are faced with a fear, try to remember a courageous dog that was able to conquer his fears with love and determination – and then follow his lead. All of us are afraid of something in our lives. There is no shame in being afraid. The key to victory, however, is to face your fear head on and do whatever it takes to overcome it. You can let your fears stop you from achieving all you want in life, or... *you can follow Caspian's lead and conquer the stairs!*

42) Use LinkedIn.com which is basically a MySpace for professionals. Include you Biz Op site in the Business website of your profile. The potential is there for hundreds – even thousands – of people to be exposed to your BIZ OP link. LinkedIn.com is free to join, but also offers upgrades for additional features.

Date, Action & Results

_____

_____

_____

_____

_____

_____

_____

43) Put a banner outside your home. The sheer gutsiness of this will draw people's attention!

Date, Action & Results

_____

_____

_____

_____

_____

44) Start a BIZ OP Team group on the web through a blog, forum or website (all of these are free). Share marketing ideas, information on products, etc. Encourage BIZ OP members to help each other. The Internet is international so you can help people no matter where in the world they live.

Date, Action & Results

_____

_____

_____

_____

_____

_____

_____

45) If you know an owner of a business, ask if you can put up a brochure stand by the cash register. Make sure to get one that takes business cards. Return frequently to replenish it!

Date, Action & Results

_____

_____

_____

_____

_____

POWER MODULE # 11

What If You're Starting From Broke?

Can you succeed with your Biz Op if you are broke or have very little resources? I believe you can but you (listen carefully if you are one of them) need to accept some basic truths in the very beginning:

1 - You are going to have to work harder than other people who have money to invest.

2 - You are going to have to be creative and think "outside-the-box" thoughts.

3 - You have to accept that it will probably take you a little longer than it will for people with money to invest.

4 - You are going to have to want it badly enough to pay a little higher price – knowing that your rewards will be exponentially greater as well!

Okay... if you are starting with nothing, or have people on your team starting with nothing, and you really want to succeed, here's where we want you to start:

Now, here are some suggestions for ways to build your business:

1 – If you don't have a computer - go to the library on a daily basis or work out a trade agreement with a neighbor to use their computer. Offer to baby sit in exchange for your computer time. Fix your specialty recipe. Do some yard work. Find something they need and do it in exchange for some regular computer time.

2 – Make absolutely sure you are receiving your company emails. They will give you a regular flow of information and inspiration that will keep you moving forward – even when you think you can't do it.

3 – Don't have a car to get to the library? Catch the bus, pull out your bike, or walk. Remember – you're going to have to work harder to make it happen but, hey, the exercise will be great for you!

4 – What to do once you're in front of the computer? Send out **Permission Emails**. Basically you are sending someone an email to ask if you can send them some information about your Biz Op. Where do you find these people? Go to your favorite search engine and search for "Free Classified Ads and Classified Ads". Then go to the ads where people are advertising for folks to join their business. The odds are that they are part of the 97% failing! Send them an email that says:

Hello _____,

I am responding to your ad I saw online. While it looks interesting I believe I have something you will be eager to know about as an additional stream of income but I want to make sure I do not SPAM anyone. The reason I'm writing is to ask you if I can send you a brief email that will introduce you to my program. I'll check out yours and you can check out mine. Sound fair?

Sincerely,

(Your name)

Now, what you CAN do is attach a banner at the bottom of your email. You are still asking permission, but you can include your Biz Op banner in your signature, or else put your Biz Op website in a signature file. Check out your own Email system to learn how to do this.

_____

5 - Send emails to people who are marketing to you!

You may learn to love SPAM and other people's Marketing emails once you read this. All of us receive emails like this every day. If you hate them right now, I would suggest this is a great time to turn lemons into lemonade! Whenever you get an email, just reply to them with an email about your Biz Op.

You'll get more tips later in the book but this should be enough to get you started. Remember, good ideas mean nothing if you don't follow up with ACTION! Determine to spend at least 1 hour a day building your Biz Op. Work online but make sure you also use all the personal, face-to-face tools we have provided for you. You need to build your business quickly so that you can get in a better financial situation. You'll want to take advantage of every tool and idea you're given!

It's up to you to come up with bright ideas to combat having very little money to build your business! The answers are there – you just have to want to find them – and then take action on them!

The movie set was ready...all actors, male, female *and* canine were present. The support staff each had their task. No one was late or out of place. Even the weather cooperated - clear skies and warm sun. The director loved this part of the production - the anticipation growing before the first shot. The excitement as months of film preparation finally became reality.

The author whose book had been adapted to the big screen was present. He got to meet the leading man and woman. The director wondered what the author thought and felt as he saw his words become real.

"John, can you come here please? We are ready to start."

John looked around and felt he was having an out-of-body experience as he watched American Hollywood celebrities, Owen Wilson and Jennifer Anniston, get ready for "take one."

"Is this my life? How did I get to this place?" John let his thoughts wander.

Amused at life's peaks and valleys, the road he now remembered had been paved with bittersweet memories.

Bittersweet really was the word that captured the process of the writing of his stories. Even his major book deal came tainted with his father's diagnosis and death from leukemia. That "joy through tears" emotion never left him.

"Ready, on the set folks! We are ready!" boomed the announcement. Silenced, the actors took their places and the cameras started rolling.

John Grogan, author of highly acclaimed *Marley and Me*, felt his dreams expand with the movie adaptation of his best seller. What started out as a therapeutic writing exercise and then a newspaper column evolved into a book phenomenon.

Marley and Me reached Number 1 on USA Today's Best-Selling Books list, selling millions of copies. John originally hoped to reach the bestseller list only *"briefly."*

Talking about his life with the "worst dog in the world," John chronicled his family's life with a yellow Labrador named Marley. The roller coaster normalcy of their lives made it easy for his readers to relate. Even with tragedy, John intertwined pure joy!

John worked 25 years in journalism before he became a "hit." He kept his dream of writing a successful novel all those years. He perfected his craft, believed in himself - and kept writing.

If you ask him for advice, guess what he says?

"Write (or do what you're passionate about) every day no matter how discouraged you get. Force yourself out of your comfort zones and do things, visit places you wouldn't otherwise... Keep a detailed journal of your daily life and use it to hone your narrative skills. More than anything, believe in yourself and your voice. Write about what you know and care passionately about... Don't write it for an agent or publisher or market niche. Write it for yourself. Write it from your heart. Write it without flinching. If you do, it will touch readers. And it will sell." (parenthesis mine)

Pretty good advice, huh? Do what you love, believe in yourself and "your voice," and keep at it.

Do it from your heart honestly, and challenge yourself to move out of the comfort of the known into the UNKNOWN.

Experience life and let others see your experiences!

46) Submit your URL to the search engines. Some of the free web submissions sites are: addme.com, accoona.com, addurlfree.com, datasoftsystem.com, scrubtheweb.com, freebyte.com, submitawebsite.com, localsubmit.com, fastsubmit.org, submitexpress.com, uswebsites.com, websitesubmit.hypermart.net, searchenginesubmission.biz, submitcorner.com, ineedhits.com.

Date, Action & Results

_____

_____

_____

_____

_____

47) If you own a business or other entity online with a customer relationship, you can offer your customers special incentives for checking out your Biz Op. The person who submitted this runs a traffic exchange online and offer my customers a FREE PRO upgrade and advertising for signing up for my other Biz Op. You really could do it for anything!

Date, Action & Results

_____

_____

_____

_____

48) Join a forum and be sure to include your BIZ OP business site in your signature. Seek out new members and welcome them to the forum. Search for topics you are familiar with and add comments. (Avoid people who are critical of others. Write their name down and do not share information with them. They tend to distort what you say and can cause problems.) When you find a topic you're good with, enter and compliment the person, express your opinion without offending anyone. Be soft and sympathetic, "I've done that and really got burned, I know how you feel." Share how you overcame your obstacle, now found a way that works, you'd be willing to share if anyone's interested. Invite them to Private Message you. Send people to your BIZ OP business site. Join forums you are passionate about. Consider joining forums in other countries! Build a rapport with people and be enthusiastic and positive.

Date, Action & Results (I'm giving you a lot of space because Forums are such a great way to connect with people. Try several...)

_____

_____

_____

_____

_____

_____

_____

_____

_____

_____

49) When going through a drive through (fast food, espresso, laundry, etc.) ask the clerk if they would like to earn some extra money. Then hand them one of your Flyers, Invitation cards or Business Cards.

Date, Action & Results

_____

_____

_____

_____

_____

_____

_____

Do you want to succeed THIS badly??

POWER MODULE # 12

More Ideas If You're "Starting from Broke"!

Starting from broke is never fun, but you'll have a better story than other people when you achieve the success you dream of! You'll also be so well equipped to help other people who feel they have no chance at fulfilling their dreams. Here are some more ideas to help you build your Biz Op without spending a penny!

Send invitations to website owners...

I love this because if you can wrap your brain around what I'm about to share, you will NEVER run out of people to share your Biz Op with. What if you were to write letters to the owners of websites?
For example... go to your favorite search engine and search for "Working From Home." You'll come up with **798,000,000 search results!** Start from the back. Start from the middle. Just start somewhere and contact the owners of these websites by going to their Contact Us Page. If you're not a writer, send them an email with a banner. Copy one of your company Invitation cards and put it in an email. Use one of your company's Email Campaign letters. Then start sending them out, telling them you visited their website and think they should see your Biz Op. You could end up with an individual or with an online business with existing massive resources to build their Biz Op – right under you!

You don't have to have a penny to be able to do this – just persistence and a will to succeed!

More Search ideas:

Women Business Owners	**8,650,000**
Teen Entrepreneur	**946,000**
Save Money	**202,000,000**
College Networks	**64,400,000**
Stay at Home moms	**7,940,000**

Come up with your own ideas – the possibilities are limitless!

Here's a sample email you can send (feel free to alter it in any way):

Hello _____,

I just explored your website and want to give you kudos on a job well done! I also want to assure you this is the only email you will receive from me. You haven't been added to a list and you won't receive other emails from me.

I'm taking the time to write because it's obvious you are committed to creating financial freedom by using the Internet as a tool. I'm sending you this email because I believe I have an exciting way for you to increase your income and create an *additional* stream of income by taking advantage of (your Biz Op.

(Brief Explanation of your Biz Op)

Check it out by watching the video at (your URL). I will work closely with you to assure your success, though the system is so simple you probably won't need me!

Have a great day!

(Your Name)
(Your Email)
(Your Phone)

Take some time today to contact at least 25 or 50 website owners. Come up with your own great ideas and create your own strategy. The opportunities in this area are virtually limitless. Whether you live in the United States, or any other country in the world, this is a strategy you can use. All it will take is some work on your part!

106

POWER STORY # 12

The testosterone filled locker room reeked of excitement, urgency and anticipation. Ankles wrapped, shoulder pads tightened, pre-game good luck routines completed, and blood pumping, the 2007 Sul Ross University Lobos prepared to storm the football field.

Nothing screams competition like West Texas football and tonight's game teemed with heightened urgency. The fans bathed in Lobo red and white chanted cheers, while the air sparkled in the arid dessert. Texas loves its football and today, Mike Flynt loved Texas.

The moment felt surreal as Mike sat facing the football field. His mind raced to embrace both his past actions and current endeavors. Only a few weeks ago he had returned to Sul Ross University to complete his senior year. His senior year! At last, he could put to death the condemning thoughts his conscience had been screaming at him.

Mike's hot temper and quicker fists ended his earlier attempts to finish this year at the school *and* on the field. Regret plagued him as disappointment followed him. His actions cost him his position as Team Captain. He had let everyone down by fighting. He had let himself down by fighting. In addition, that feeling of "I want to finish what I started" nagged his every thought.

"Mike Flynt!" boomed the announcer as the crowd went berserk.

Having been kicked off the football team and out of school, Mike had finished his undergraduate degree by taking classes elsewhere. Yet, the star football player in him never, ever lost the desire to take the field again with his team.

But those weeks of deep regret slowly evolved into months, then years, and then decades. DECADES of grief over his past failure still plagued him.

Thirty-six years later, at fifty-nine years old - yes, 59 years old - Mike returned to Sul Ross and finished what he had started but lost. Mike waited 36 years to have the courage to return to the field. He never lost his dream to play that last semester of football.

An impromptu "reunion" of teammates rekindled that flickering flame. A quick check into his eligibility revealed he was, in fact, STILL eligible to return to collegiate play. A very lengthy conversation with his wife (and their real estate agent) prompted the move from Nashville, Tennessee to Alpine, Texas. A few more lengthy conversations (and workouts) with the coaches at the university, resulted in Mike taking the field for the Lobos during the 2007 season.

At 59, Mike was in tiptop physical. He had worked professionally as a strength and conditioning coach for two major universities... and invented a piece of exercise equipment that led to his own fitness company. He had kept his body in top shape through the years, as he married, had children and then celebrated the arrival of a grandchild.

Pretty amazing!

His former buddies encouraged him to "give it a shot." They nicknamed themselves the "Sul Ross Baby Boomers" and became Mike's official fan club.

His wife encouraged her husband to do what he wanted to!

The current coaches who at first said, *"he's an idiot,"* changed their minds and said, *"He is in great physical condition. He still runs a 5-flat 40 and bench-presses I-don't-know-what. He's a specimen for 59 years old."*

I could understand their initial hesitancy. Not only was he a grandfather, but also a card-carrying member of AARP, eight years older than his coach, had two kids older than any of his teammates AND was only 6 years away from qualifying for Medicare.

More than just playing football, his wife and family knew that pursuing his dream on the field again would lift the black cloud of regret from his life.

"There are not many times in life when you have an opportunity to go back and right a wrong...I want to play, but at the same time, I want to help these young men; to make up for some young men I let down 36 years ago. I told (my wife) for me to know that I can do it and not do it would be worse than losing out the first time."

Those are some great thoughts from Mike Flynt. The next time you think it is too late to follow your dreams, think of Mike. He never let go of the dream of playing again.

While you might not want to play collegiate football; perhaps it is writing a book, creating art, opening a restaurant, moving to the beach, asking forgiveness, paying a debt, or taking responsibility. Whatever it is - it is never too late to try.

I want to encourage you today. Take a step. Then take another. If you can't do it all, then do what you can. I know that the longer we put off doing what we know is right, the harder it is to initiate action. So do not wait any longer.

Make a list today of what it is you want to do... and then make serious effort to begin making that list a reality.

So yeah... let's make that list. RIGHT NOW!

_____

_____

_____

_____

_____

_____

_____

_____

_____

_____

50) Set up a My Space page just for your BIZ OP. There are groups, forums, classifieds, and other places where you can advertise on My Space.

Date, Action & Results

_____

_____

_____

_____

_____

_____

51) Park your car on or near a college/university campus and talk to students passing by. Ask: "Excuse me, could you use some extra income?" Or "So you know any students who could use some extra income?" If they are receptive or curious at all, hand them a flyer, brochure, etc. Now granted, this can be rather intimidating for shy people so it might not be your thing. On the other hand, if you push yourself you might be very surprised by the results. You could perhaps tell yourself to try it for just one hour and see what happens...

Date, Action & Results

_____

_____

_____

_____

52) If there is a great sale through your BIZ OP, post it in one of the groups you belong to or write a blog about it. Highlight the special deal or opportunity and then give your link so they can go directly to your website and either buy product or sign up.

Date, Action & Results

_____

_____

_____

_____

_____

_____

_____

53) Put a sign in the back window of your car for all to see at stop signs, stop lights, stop-and-go traffic, parking lots, etc. Include your domain name and something simple like: Shop, Save and Make Money. Or... Lose Weight Easily! And be sure to have Invitation Cards, flyers or Business Cards in your car at all times to hand out!

Date, Action & Results

_____

_____

_____

_____

_____

_____

More "Starting From Broke" ideas!

Here's another great idea!

Contact Ezine owners

An Ezine is nothing more than a magazine online, and they support themselves by selling advertising. Since you're broke you're not going to buy advertising but there is still a way to approach them. *Try the following email:*

Hello _____,

I have checked out your advertising but I think what I have to share with you is much more valuable than me just buying an Ad. We have many Ezine owners who are becoming members of (your Biz Op.) Instead of making a mere _____ (cost of ad) from me you could be generating unlimited income. If only 1% of your readership took you up on getting involved with (your Biz Op) your income would be astounding. That's why so many Ezine owners are choosing to get started now.

Check it out by watching the video at (your URL). I'll work closely with you to assure your success though you'll find the system so simple you probably won't need me!

Have a great day!

(Your Name)
(Your email)

_____

What kind of ezine can you approach? The better question is who **can't** you approach? Doesn't everyone have everyday needs and wants? Doesn't everyone have a desire for greater financial freedom? There is no limit.

Contact Websites with Newsletters

While there are lots of websites that don't have ezines that sell advertising, there are millions that offer newsletters to their members. These cover thousands of retail outlets, service professions, etc. Think plumbers, electricians, landscapers, interior designers, etc.

The first thing you want to do is subscribe to as many newsletters as you can. Sure, they may clog up your email box but I think you'll learn to appreciate it! ☺ Once you have received your first newsletter – and READ IT! - send them this reply:

Hello _____,

I just read your latest newsletter and really enjoyed it. Especially the article about _____. I have something to share with you that I believe your readers will really benefit from.

(You need to write a blurb about your Biz Op. Go through company literature to find what will work most effectively.)

It would take you just minutes to integrate it in with your existing website and generate unlimited income.

Check it out by watching the video at (your URL). I'll work closely with you to assure your success though you'll find the system so simple you probably won't need me!

Have a great day!

(Your Name)
(Your email)

If you're creative and willing to think "Outside the Box" there is no limit to the approaches you can take in contacting people. Via email, it won't cost you a penny. How many emails can you send daily? 50? 100? How badly do you want Financial Freedom? Even if you're a single Mom with 5 kids, you can find time to send even 2-3 emails. Added up on a daily basis you will send hundreds – giving you a chance to create financial freedom.

You've discovered the Biz Op you believe will work for you. Now it's up to you to actually use these ideas to create the Financial Freedom you dream of.

Here are some more valuable tips:

Focus on finding people with money to spend

This one is really important. While you will want to share your Biz Op with everyone you know – giving them a chance for success as well – you want to put your focus (at least in the beginning) on people who have money to spend – people who can afford to buy your products or services, and pay the membership fees. You can only make money when the people on your team are able to generate Income. If you build your team with only people who are in the same financial straits you are, you will have a large team, but you won't make as much money!

If you think you can't communicate with people who have a lot of money until you have a lot of your own, I want you to RUN to your local video store and get the movie *The Pursuit of Happyness*, starring Will Smith. It's a true story about a man who beat the odds – earning a place in a Wall Street investment firm while he was living in a Homeless Shelter. Whatever your current condition, you CAN change it! Set a night aside and watch this movie – alone, with your partner, or with your kids. It will be powerful for all of you!

Spend time on your Local college campus.

The 18-24 age group consists of some of the most motivated people around. Just think how much debt most of them are leaving college with! They grew up on the Internet and do almost everything online. Find them! Hand out Invitation cards. Print up some flyers – all in black & white if you can't afford color. Call around till you find one of the places that will print them for 3 cents apiece, or do them on your own printer.

Put up flyers around campus. Leave them in bathrooms. Again, be creative. The only limit is what you're willing to do to change your life!

Swirling paint and oils lay before her, each one beckoning to be used. Choosing the precise color stemmed from a lifelong love affair with art. McKenzie paused, breathed and continued her creation. Focused on the canvas before her, she gazed at the soothing colors like a mother gazes over her newborn. Rich terra cotta, rippling azure, and sun kissed goldenrod, waited to be splashed onto her canvas. Paintbrush in hand, frozen in mid air, McKenzie stopped.

Eyes shut; she willed the headache to leave her.

Breathing deeply, the fumes invaded her head and made the throbbing pain intensify. Her years in the studio flashed before her own mind's canvas. Paintings, awards, TV spotlights, celebrity buyers, galleries, art shows, fundraisers, and numerous accolades swept over her as she tried to relax.

Her current work deserved attention. She needed to rest. A few more cleansing breaths and the pain seemed to settle to a dull ache. Shifting her weight from left to right foot, McKenzie bent, and decided that the rippling azure fit best into her newly formed stream. McKenzie wondered what was wrong with her body.

The next day, her doctor turned and looked at the artist. Her bold blonde hair enhanced by the clarity of her direct gaze made his information more difficult.

"McKenzie, you have Lupus...an autoimmune disease that can affect various parts of the body, including the skin, joints, heart, lungs, blood, kidneys and brain. The immune system cannot tell the difference between foreign substances and its own cells and tissues. It then makes antibodies directed against itself. These antibodies cause inflammation, pain and damage in various parts of the body. We believe it is linked to your years of exposure to the fumes and solvents from your mixed media art."

Taking a deep breath, McKenzie placed the printed information in her purse, nodded at her return appointment date, and walked out of the doctor's office in a daze.

"Okay, I know I have Lupus. I also know I have to paint. Well, I'll just figure a way to do both. I guess that means I create new art products... products that don't create havoc on the artists, or the environment. We can do it... I don't know exactly how just yet, but... I've got to find a way. Art is my life."

McKenzie realized she had to find a way to avoid the toxic materials she breathed as she poured life into her art. Resolved to find help, for her as well as for a toxin-free creative arena for all artists, McKenzie got into her car a bit sad, a lot wiser, and incredibly motivated to make a difference in her world.

This motivation led her and her art team to create the very first environmentally friendly art supplies!

Leadership Energy in Environmental Design (an organization directed by the United States Green Building Council) deems all her art products completely compliant with their standards. These products are the very first in the world! *'GREEN'* art products now exist in every stage of her mediums... from canvas to frames. McKenzie has dedicated her life to art and now that dedication encompasses art that makes a difference!

A quick look at her website reveals unusual descriptions, *"Handmade Organic Paper! Eco-Friendly Inks! Recycled Frames! Even Our Printer is Green!"*

"Promoting Global Awareness through ART" is her mission. *"We can change the world in more ways than just changing our light bulbs and recycling our water bottles. [McKenzie] creates art that saves the planet... She gives 100% of the proceeds of her eco art away to organizations working to save the planet too."*

Artist McKenzie is known as the "Hollywood Charity Artist" because her heart is as generous as her art collectors are famous. Top Hollywood celebrities willingly wait two years for her new award winning creations. Her passion to

express her world is her lifeblood. Lupus did not stop this woman, and her accolades, opportunities, and awards actually increased as she honestly let the art world know of her struggle with Lupus and her commitment to "going green."

"I draw my inspiration from the changing patterns and environments in which I surround

myself... I create forms and shapes – colors and hues – to convey energy and movement... I strive for new ways to represent my physical and spiritual sensations in paint. Vibrant and intense color is integral to my compositions. Energy is the underlying theme of my work. I strive to paint with honesty those things which move me."

Let's attempt to follow McKenzie's success. Take whatever life throws at us and find a creative path. Don't let your goals change because an obstacle or a detour looms. Determine to see your dreams become reality.

I love McKenzie's attitude (and her artwork)! She gives back to the world as she does what she loves! She is both immensely successful AND making an enormous difference to the planet!

What a way to live – what a way to GIVE!

Go color your world your way! What obstacles and detours are hampering your progress? What can you do to change that reality?

_____

_____

_____

_____

_____

_____

_____

_____

_____

_____

54) Contact web site owners (through their contact forms). You can choose web sites that are already offering different work from home or business opportunities. Use your local phone book and look for businesses that have web sites (and or email addresses) listed. *Then just send them an email and ask them to check you out!*

Date, Action & Results

---

55) Ask friends or relatives who have web sites to put one of your BIZ OP banners on their site. If they're willing to do this, then they will probably be willing to join. If they are not, and you get good results from the banner, you should re-approach them, tell them you don't want them to miss out and offer your Biz Op to them again. Maybe they just need proof it works!

Date, Action & Results

---

56) Don't forget free radio, newspaper and TV advertising. And add new methods daily. Collaborate with your teammates wherever possible.

Date, Action & Results

_____

_____

_____

_____

_____

_____

_____

57) Run free ads on craigslist.org. You will need to get a domain name (these are very inexpensive) to link from (otherwise affiliate type URLs are automatically deleted). Place your ads in the "services" section under "small business" ads or they'll be flagged and deleted. You won't be able to run too many ads on the same day in too many cities.

Date, Action & Results

_____

_____

_____

_____

_____

POWER MODULE # 14

Honesty Is The BEST Policy!

I want to talk about something very serious. *Telling the truth.* Do you know why a lot of people have a negative perception of *any* Home-Based Business? It's because they were brought in to a company in the past by people telling them they could make huge money right away. They were told there was really nothing to it; that it would require no significant effort, and no major time investment.

Wrong!

Let me paint a scenario that happens every day. Someone is brought into a business by someone telling them they are already making big money after just a few months – when they're not. The new person is extremely excited and jumps in right away, already thinking about how they are going to spend all the money. They work hard for a few months, don't achieve the same "fake income", and then drop out because it must not work for them. They figure all home-based businesses are the same. All you did by lying was set them up for failure. *How sad...*

The truth is this. Any business will take work. Those who achieve high incomes will apply themselves diligently to succeed. Home-based business rewards are commensurate with effort. You *will* have to work!

Yes, it is important to let people know the potential of your business. You can share figures with them so they know just what their efforts can produce. Your company presentation does this for you. But can you guarantee they will make that kind of money? No. You can show them what they *can* make but only their effort and work will determine what they *will* make. Be sure to make that clear to them. Do not make this seem like an easy thing. It's not. It may be incredibly SIMPLE, but it still requires effort.

Maybe you've been told to *"Fake it till you make it."* You've been told to make yourself seem like you are a success before you are. Let me be blunt – that's lying. And it won't help anyone - including you. It's terrible to walk around with the pressure of what your team and other people will think if they find out you're not wildly successful yet, that you're still working another job, or that you're struggling financially. *For what?!*

There's nothing wrong with saying, *"I just got started, too. We'll be in this thing together. Let's watch the company presentation again so we're reminded of the potential."*

There's nothing wrong with saying, *"Yes, I had a really tough day today – 2 people told me no. But that's okay because they can't keep me down. I'm determined to do whatever it takes to succeed."* Then go do it!

The people you are working with will appreciate you so much because they don't have to carry the burden of being fake either! You can learn, grow and succeed together!

It *is* true that absolutely anyone can succeed in a home-based business – as long as you have great products and a great company. There is nothing that would exclude you from being able to achieve financial freedom – nothing but a lack of effort on your part. The sky is the limit if you want it badly enough.

Anyone can succeed, but it is important to paint a realistic picture. First for yourself – then for the people you bring in. Understating the hard work and perseverance to achieve great success is the most often utilized strategy by those who create false expectations. Most people will quickly see through the false promises in a very short time and then quit. Too often, people drop out because they weren't told the truth in the first place. How sad.

While a legitimate home-based business is not a get-rich quick scheme, it is definitely an opportunity for people to achieve all their goals if they will discipline themselves in a consistent way and learn the simple skills necessary to succeed. It is your job to communicate that clearly.

Most people want to be able to quit their jobs and let their new business take care of them. Great! But what is it really going to take? Very few people can come into a home-based business full time right at the beginning. They are going to have to continue to work their regular job, working hard until their business income replaces their current income. Make sure they know that. Give them the truth.

"You know, _____, the truth is it's only those who treat it like a profession who get to the big money. Give it all your energy and you'll naturally get there sooner. Undertake it part-time, and stay with it steadily, and you'll get there eventually. But there is no way for you to earn big money by exerting only minimal effort. You have two choices. If it is possible for you to work full time by tightening your belt and living off money you have now, great! Go for it full time. Your other option (which is the one most people will have to take) is to work very aggressively part time until you've replaced your income and then go full-time. Whatever way you decide to do, it is great! I'll help you any way I can."

Let people make their decision from a place of reality. It will assure you don't have an angry, dissatisfied team member further down the road.

Don't tell people they only need to talk to a few people to make huge money. What if all those people say no? What if they have to talk to lots of people before someone says yes? What if they drop out because you gave them the wrong impression – before they find the people that say yes, the ones who will build their business for them?

Shoot straight. *"You're going to have to contact a lot of people. You're going to have to move out of your comfort zone. You are going to have to deal with people saying no. But I'll be there with you. I'll be there for you. And if you hang with it you'll build a business that will give you the freedom you need."*

You've told them the truth. You also told them to hang in there – that it will be worth it. They believe you and hang in there. Now you both win!

Decide at the beginning to be honest. It will benefit you. It will benefit those you bring on. Make your own commitments to success. Help those you bring on to make their commitments – then be there with them every step of the way!!

POWER STORY # 14

The radio station receptionist looked up. Before her, guitar in hand, stood a young man with clear blue eyes, a sincere smile, and a slight drawl.

"Good morning, sir. How can I help you?"

"Good morning. My name is John. I am the songwriter for Peter, Paul and Mary's recent hit, 'Leaving on a Jet Plane.' I'd like to interview and perhaps sing a couple other songs I've written. I'm doing a concert here Friday night at the Community Club Room."

"Well, wait right here and I'll talk to the station manager... but I think we have time for you. Hang on."

John sat and waited on the cool black couch, strumming his guitar, tuning its strings, and humming softly as he warmed up his voice. He expected they'd let him play and he aimed to give them a good solid mini-concert. Excited in his mind for the potential of this interview and the concert, still he stifled a yawn.

"Guess I am a little tired," he thought.

This self-tour, although critically important to his career, seemed lonely at times. Always knocking on cold doors, and working day and night to get his name and voice before the people was grueling. Yet living his dreams stirred emotions deep within his soul. Accused of being a profound thinking, intensely feeling kind of guy, John accepted that truth and set his yearnings to music.

"Sir? If you can wait 15 minutes, the D.J. would love to talk to you and have you play. Can I get you some coffee or water while you wait? I'd enjoy it if you'd keep playing, you have such a mellow peaceful sound... I like it."

Taking the offered water, John Denver smiled, settled back in the waiting area, and began his long wonderful career of entertaining the world with his melodic, thought provoking, feel-good tunes!

As a boy, John was given a guitar by his grandmother to help him overcome his shyness. She believed in her grandson and wanted more for his life.

Soon he began etching out songs. Traveling alone for many years, he dreamed of performing and changing the world with his music. And he did.

For over three decades before his accidental death in 1997, John lived his music. John lived his dreams.

He entertained presidents in countries the world round, explored nearly every continent in the world while giving concerts, recorded and released hit records time and time again. When he fell in love with the earth and its environmental issues; he lent his name, his money, and his folk hero iconic status to its causes, thus helping preserve the bounty of the world.

However, in the beginning when John's dream was simply a young man's dream, he took opportunity wherever he found it to step out. He told a television talk show host that he *"refused to **not** take advantage of every opportunity made available for him to grow as an artist and a more complete entertainer."*

Leaving Texas and moving to California, he at first played underground music clubs until he auditioned for, and won, a spot in a folk music trio. His four years with this trio became the springboard for his remarkable solo career.

While John may have left this earth, his spirit remains in his music and with his family and fans. His sincerity toward people and the earth set him apart in the music industry where jealousy, greed and skepticism run rampant. His dreams live on and we are better people for having listened.

And listen we have! John received over 17 Grammies, Emmys, American Music Awards, Country Music Association awards, Academy of Country Music awards, and other major music awards, including Poet Laureate of Colorado. His music still gives generations of listeners peace, hope and joy. John Denver has nearly 100 songs, albums, and compilations to his credit. The total count of sales *exceeds* 30 million albums.

And watch John we have...with over 60 films, television specials, documentaries and made- for-TV movies, John was no stranger to the spotlight in any form.

John's success came about because his grandmother believed in him and encouraged him.

He subsequently embraced her encouragement, faced and overcame his shyness, and believed he could live his dreams. He even knocked on doors asking for an audience. Eventually, he hit success because he didn't give up!

And the world came to be profoundly blessed by this unique troubadour.

Watch your thoughts, they become words.
Watch your words, they become actions.

Watch your actions, they become habits.
Watch your habits, they become character.
Watch your character, it becomes your destiny!

58) After you've added 10 (or whatever your magic # is) to your team, start helping those ten give away their ten. Work with the willing and make it a win-win situation for everyone. *That doesn't mean you quit adding to your own frontline!*

Date, Action & Results

_____

_____

_____

_____

_____

_____

59) Read the newspaper for articles in which people are helping other people. Get their website, email address, phone number, address, whatever information you can find in order to contact them about BIZ OP. Do the same thing while watching TV (for commercials) or the nightly news.

Date, Action & Results

_____

_____

_____

_____

_____

60) Get interviewed by someone who writes for a Home Biz newsletter. Ask them if they would like to profile an exciting business. Tell them why it's so great and they may just want to profile you. This is great free advertising!

Date, Action & Results

_____

_____

_____

_____

_____

_____

61) Whatever you choose to do, be consistent. Post on forums, hand out business cards and talk about BIZ OP everywhere you go. But you've got to do it consistently, not hit-or-miss. That's the key to success.

Date, Action & Results

_____

_____

_____

_____

_____

POWER MODULE #15

Being A Great Leader!

Bringing someone into your Business is just the beginning. Every business is set up differently. You may be responsible for training and providing tools – perhaps your company does that. Regardless, it's up to YOU to provide them encouragement & support. It's up to you to become a Great Leader!

No matter what company you represent, the basic premise of Leadership is very simple – people will do what you are doing. If you're building your team, they will build. If you're buying and using your product or service, they will too. You need to look at yourself every day and determine if you are the person you want your team to copy... The most important thing you want to determine at the beginning is if you want to be a Sponsor or a Recruiter. Let's take a look at the difference...

Are you a recruiter? Or are you a sponsor?

There is a big difference.

A recruiter is effective at "signing up" people, and then moving on to "sign up" others. The recruiter seems to be in a frantic search to find superstars among the crowd, and their way to "find" them is to "sign them up" and then watch and wait. The recruiter believes in "love 'em and leave 'em." He expects the superstars to eventually rise to the top, and the others to eventually quit.

The sponsor has a different attitude. He believes that any person worth sponsoring is worth developing. The sponsor believes in "marrying" the people he sponsors. The recruiter believes in the "one-night-stand."

Being a sponsor is an ongoing, continuing activity. It is this ongoing activity that creates loyalty to the sponsor, and gives the sponsor serious credibility. The recruiter is a traveling salesman; once he has sold you, he is gone. The sponsor is a helper/teacher who wants you to have the training and tools you need to be successful, and the encouragement to keep plugging. There is also a transferable concept here. Your sponsor wants you to be a sponsor.

A sponsor develops other sponsors by deliberate, careful help and encouragement. A recruiter expects a born superstar.

Think about all the children in a hospital nursery. They each have a card that reads either "boy" or "girl." Not one of those cards read "superstar." Superstars are "made," they are not "born." They are "developed." Making a superstar takes training, encouragement, help, patience, and time. It takes being a sponsor.

What does it take to become a superstar? It takes a lot of attitude-type things, such as confidence, commitment, determination, credibility, etc. Where do these "attitude" type things come from? They are learned. They are taught. They are "caught." Here are the stages of the development of a superstar.

1. Learn to be a real sponsor.

2. Develop others who will be real sponsors.

3. Teach them to teach others to be real sponsors.

The secret to success is found in this: the recruiter is not building a "multi-level" organization, it is all one level (and most of them will quit). The sponsor is building a duplicable system that can run downline through his organization. This builds a powerful team because it is built deep and strong.

What is the difference between a recruiter and a sponsor? It is the difference between "hype" and "help." The sponsor's job begins when you enroll; the recruiter's job is done when you enroll. The goal of the recruiter is to sign up people. The goal of the sponsor is to train leaders. Before asking yourself which you want to be, ask yourself which do you want your upline to be. Remember, you are the upline to other people. The key to success in your home-based business is found in Two rules:

1. Be a sponsor.

2. Keep being a sponsor.

*   *   *   *   *   *   *   *   *   *

Here are some tips to make you a great Leader:

• Send a personal email to everyone who joins on your front line. Welcome them, give them your contact information and let them know you are available to help them if they want or need it. (Keep track of how you're doing...)

_____

_____

_____

_____

_____

_____

_____

_____

_____

_____

_____

_____

_____

_____

_____

- Set up a GROUP through your email provider. Each time someone new joins beneath you, add them to your Group. That way you only have to send one email to your entire team. Just make sure you put the Group name in BCC (Blind Carbon Copy) so that everyone's email address doesn't show up – email courtesy.

If you do this make sure you provide a way for them to opt out of receiving them. All you have to do is add one line at the bottom that says, "If you don't wish to receive these emails, just send me back a reply that says Remove. I will do so immediately!"

Yes – I set up my Group! _____

- If you would like a more robust Email System, set up an AutoResponder system. I recommend a good one in this book. It may be what you are looking for.

- Touch base with your frontline weekly and remind them you're available. You may also want to share how your own team is growing. Sometimes all they need is encouragement. Schedule it onto your calendar so you don't forget.

Yes – I scheduled it on my calendar! _____

- The best thing you can do to keep your team growing rapidly is to lead by example. If you are signing up new members, so will they. It's really pretty simple.

- Let your team know when you have great results from your product or service. They all need to see the positive results of what they are promoting. Keep track of your results. (You'll be so glad you did!)

_____

_____

_____

_____

_____

_____

_____

_____

_____

_____

_____

_____

_____

_____

_____

_____

_____

- If you have Tips to share with them, please do. (Again, you'll be glad you keep the tips you share!)

_____

_____

_____

_____

_____

_____

_____

_____

_____

_____

_____

_____

_____

_____

_____

_____

_____

Keep an eye on your entire team through your Genealogy Report (most companies today provide them in your back office on the Internet). You can send emails directly to people just by clicking on their email address. When someone brings on their first new member, send them an email to congratulate them. As their team is growing, send them more emails to congratulate them. Let them know you are aware of their efforts.

"Ah, Sunday mornings! The day of rest. Sacred. I love it!"

Susan's thoughts floated as lightly as the wispy clouds she watched out her bedroom window as she readied for another church service.

"I wonder how many people will be there today? Not that it matters. I play for God and to help God's people."

An hour later, Susan settled behind the organ at the African Methodist Episcopal church in Brooklyn. The fifth of seven children, Susan dreamed big dreams. She loved playing the organ and soothing the spirits of her listeners, yet her true passion lay outside music.

Susan longed to heal the body. She dreamed of studying medicine and having her own clinic.

The profitable pig farm her parents owned gave her privileges not everyone enjoyed. She knew the elite society of Brooklyn, yet her heart remained open to everyone. Susan also knew she could handle the rigorous studies of medicine if she could only gain acceptance into school.

By the end of the month, she should receive notification of her status. Until then, she would play the organ and dream.

The year was 1867.

Susan Smith, 20, became the first African American woman in New York and

only the third African American woman in the entire U.S., to enter medicine when she gained acceptance as a student at New York Medical College.

"Think she can handle it?" the young man in the first desk sneered at Susan as she walked into the classroom.

"She's a woman! I doubt it," came the sarcastic reply from his colleague.

"And she's black! Wonder why they let her in?" mocked a third.

Such rude behavior had no effect on Susan. Growing accustomed to narrow minds and deep prejudice, she ignored the shallow heckling.

Susan concentrated instead on her studies.

Highly intelligent and deeply devoted, she focused on learning all she could. A sponge for knowledge, Susan thrived in the world of academia. She proved to the outside world what she had known all along - that a woman could succeed in medicine as easily as a man.

In just three years, amidst daily jeers, taunts, skepticism, criticism, and apathy, Susan graduated *valedictorian* of her class!!

Using compassion, and dignity, Dr. McKinney (changing her name upon marriage) opened her first practice in her Brooklyn home and soon established herself as a competent, knowledgeable and empathetic physician. Her patients spanned both socioeconomic and racial lines as she treated the whole person. Her practice grew steadily as did her reputation as a very talented pediatrician.

By the end of her life in 1918, Dr. McKinney-Steward (hyphenating her name after becoming a widow and remarrying) would accomplish many diverse professional goals.

Among them would be:

- Opening two private medical clinics
- Co-founding the Women's Royal Union of New York
- Participating in the King's County Homeopathic Society
- Co-founding the Women's Hospital and Dispensary in Brooklyn (which later became the Memorial Hospital for Women and Children)
- Serving on the staff of her alma mater, New York Medical College
- Supervising the Home for Aged Colored People
- Serving as college physician at Wilberforce University in Ohio

Dr. McKinney-Steward set out to do what few women had ever done.

She entered a male-dominated profession and flourished!

Think what would have happened if she'd accepted the limits society tried to place on her. Her dreams of living the life of a physician could easily have been thwarted had she listened to the naysayers of the times. Dr. McKinney-Steward loved playing the organ, yet she wanted to make another kind of difference in the world. Even after she married and began practicing medicine, she continued playing the organ at her church. She managed to accomplish her medical dreams *and* grow her musical talents.

I am so glad she did not listen to the ignorance of those times. She played an extremely crucial part in the educational process of African American women in the U.S. as well as in the medical field.

Today as you look around at *your* obstacles and negative remarks, remember Susan McKinney-Steward and follow her example. Focus on your dreams and reject any criticism. Live your life your way and let your passions be your guide. Dr. Susan McKinney-Steward overcame incredible odds to pursue her passions. You can too!

"The truth is that our finest moments are most likely to occur when we are feeling deeply uncomfortable, unhappy, or unfulfilled. For it is only in such moments, propelled by our discomfort, that we are likely to step out of our ruts and start searching for different ways or truer answers."

62) Send an email to people who are advertising online and offer them BIZ OP for free. No matter what they are currently doing, BIZ OP can be part of their strategy for gaining financial freedom. Of course include your domain name or BIZ OP business site URL.

Date, Action & Results

_____

_____

_____

_____

_____

_____

_____

63) Use your Ebay "About Me" page to peak curiosity. (If you aren't already a member of Ebay, it's very easy and free to sign up.) You can cut and paste advertisements from your BIZ OP back office or use banners or ecards or anything else that makes it look attractive and inviting. DO NOT try to sell BIZ OP on your About Me page, just get people interested and curious. Now, under your favorite links, put a link to your BIZ OP business page. Once you have your About Me page set up and looking the way you want it, start looking at the Ebay groups. There are thousands of groups out there that you can join. Look for ones that interest you. As you are looking, notice the date of the last posting. If it's more than a couple weeks old, it's not an active group so look for others. An active group will have people sharing their wares, just talking or even asking for help. When you first join, tell a little about yourself and what you do. Don't try to sell BIZ OP. Just get acquainted first. You might insert a picture of the BIZ OP logo or a banner from your back office on one of your next posts. It will arouse curiosity and someone will probably ask what it is or ask for information. Don't offer any information in the post, but send them to your About Me page and tell them to click on the link in your Favorite Links section. Ebay has a very strict rule about posting links directly to other sites. They have a 2-click rule. If a person has to click on 2 links to get where you want them, it's okay. One click is a no-no so be very careful. The more groups you join the better. Just be sure you play by Ebay's rules.

Date, Action & Results

_____

_____

_____

_____

_____

_____

_____

_____

64) If you know people in MLM companies, share your Biz Op with them. The days are gone when people are doing just one business exclusively. There is great value in multiple streams of income. It's smart for people to leverage what they have already built, or start another stream. Successful people are always looking for ways to increase their success.

Date, Action & Results

_____

_____

_____

_____

_____

_____

_____

_____

_____

_____

_____

65) Listen to your company owner or Trainer because they know what they are talking about. Study the training in the back office; take notes and apply it. Most important – make a plan, any plan, and make sure you follow it. If you are shy and doubtful, set some easy goals and track your success.

Date, Action & Results

_____

_____

_____

_____

_____

_____

_____

_____

POWER MODULE # 16

More On Being A Great Leader!

Many people today are building their business primarily through the Internet. While I hope going through this book will balance your efforts with real people connections, the power of the Internet is not to be denied. Here are some things to consider:

Are you a Proactive Leader? Are you contacting every person on your team to welcome them and offer help? If you are, you're definitely on the right track. Even if they never need your help, they know you are there and that they aren't alone.

One of the potential hazards of having an Internet Business is that it can become too impersonal. *You never talked to them to get them signed up, so why should you talk to them now?* For one simple reason. Every member who signs up through the Internet is a **PERSON** – with real dreams, and a real life, and real reasons for joining your business opportunity. Don't you want to know what they are? And wouldn't you like to know someone cared enough about you to simply send an email, snail mail or make a call?

Be a Proactive leader. It will do wonders for your business!

You can also hold a Contest for your own team. While your company probably has contests going on, there is nothing to keep you from having your own contests – offering prizes for the most people added, and other prizes based on sales.

Think about doing a contest for your team. It's not what they win – it's the fun of winning! And because people love to win, it is motivation for them to build their team – building YOUR team as well.

Here are some prize ideas:

- Certificates (you can make them yourself)
- Starbucks Cards
- Create a website and post their pictures
- Gift Cards
- Buy them a meal at their own local restaurant

- Have a pizza delivered to their house
- Be creative and come up with some of your own ideas...

Being a Leader is great fun. You will meet many amazing people through My Power Mall and will build some great relationships. And, the stronger your team is, the more secure your income will be!

Keep track of any contests you have:

_____

_____

_____

_____

_____

_____

_____

_____

_____

_____

_____

_____

_____

The breakfast crowd at the diner was lively and upbeat.

Bearing platters of eggs, toast, hash browns and steaming java, Suze wished she could match their enthusiasm. Too many cares and concerns pushed her down. Her bright blue eyes and flash of a smile belied her despondent attitude as she waitressed.

"Excuse me, may we have more coffee please?"

"Sure. Be right there."

"Suze? What is wrong? For years you've been serving me breakfast and I've never seen you so down."

Glancing down at Howard, a customer of 6 years, Suze turned to snatch the coffee pot. Looking back at her trusted customer, she hesitated.

So many experiences from her life came to her mind. She wanted to tell him about sitting in the last row in the last seat in elementary school because she couldn't read or speak very well. She wanted to share the humiliation of being tagged the "dumbest" girl in school - every school - not just elementary school. She had the same label in high school and college, too. She thought about admitting her premature exodus from college without her bachelor's degree. She'd left school because she was too afraid to study a foreign language. For a moment, she wondered if he would believe her if, she recounted her months of living in her van because she was homeless.

Instead, what came out her mouth went something like this: *"Well, Howard, I want to open my own restaurant. I have a dream. I asked my parents for $20,000 to help but of course, they don't have that kind of money. I'll be ok. Just sad. Let me get your coffee."*

What happened next astounded Suze. When Howard came to pay for his breakfast, he left checks and financial commitments he'd gathered from all the customers totaling $50,000 with a note that read: ***"THIS IS FOR PEOPLE LIKE YOU, SO THAT YOUR DREAMS CAN COME TRUE. TO BE PAID BACK IN TEN YEARS, IF YOU CAN, WITH NO INTEREST.***"

Sitting her tray down, Suze looked at Howard in utter and complete amazement.

"Howard, thank you. Thank all of you. But are these checks going to bounce like mine do?"

Howard smiled gently and answered, *"No. Take them to Merrill Lynch down the street and put the money in a money market account."*

Totally confused now, Suze stopped Howard before he walked out the door. *"Howard, what is Merrill Lynch and what does a money market account do?"*

Have you heard of Suze Orman? Read her best-selling books? Heard her speak? Taken her expert financial advice?

If so, then you know this once down-and-out waitress encountered a rocky road before realizing her dreams!

Did you know that initial $50,000 gift was swindled away from her? She lost every penny!

So what did she do?

With courage and fear, she secured a job as a novice broker at the same Merrill Lynch branch, sued them as the company that allowed her broker to cheat her, won the lawsuit, received her $50,000 WITH interest, and eventually paid off her breakfast cafe investors.

But it wasn't easy.

Suffering outright ridicule, criticism, and skepticism, Suze faced down her critics every day at work.

As a broker, she remembers eating *alone* at a very inexpensive fast food restaurant every day for lunch while the other brokers went to upscale restaurants. The year was 1980. She drove a 1967 Volvo station wagon, and parked on the street because she couldn't afford to park in the paid parking lot. The other brokers drove BMWs, Mercedes Benzes and Jaguars.

Suze never lets go of her humble background.

Her story of fame and fortune tempers the real riches of her life. She always teaches the same lesson: never forget the *people* in your life. Her award

winning TV program always ends with the same slogan, *"People first, then money, then things,"* reminding us that without people in our lives, we are nothing.

Today Ms. Suze Orman is: a financial expert; best selling author; popular public speaker; award-winning acclaimed television personality (and former homeless waitress) worth over $10 million and living her dreams every day!

Can you imagine your name substituted in the sentence above? Can you imagine living your wildest dreams?

I believe if you can envision it, you can make it happen.

Today as you, dream...dream big. Believe you can live your dreams. Vow to get up each day and take one little step toward your dreams. It is no disgrace to fail – just be sure to get up and get started again. As Suze says, *"I'll never forget the man who believed in me, who helped me put aside my shame and rewrite the story history had handed me."*

People first.

Then money.

Then things.

66) Do a search on your favorite search engine for lists of organizations. For instance, type in: contact dog rescue shelters email list (then substitute charter schools, children charities, online businesses, whatever) in your search. Look for lists, for example: akc.org/breeds/rescue.cfm or animal-link.org. You're looking for lots of contact names and email addresses all on one page. You can also put a state name in your search. This saves you from searching one website at a time. Cut and paste the email address into your email, then cut/paste you email message (save it to a document so you can get to it quickly), then add the person's name or the name of the organization.

Date, Action & Results

_____

_____

_____

_____

_____

_____

67) Do a 1-2 minute home video and post it on YouTube. Your friends will be impressed with your bravery. ☺ They'll be willing to watch this, when they may not have been willing to hear it another way. Plus – you never know if it might go viral on you!

Date, Action & Results

_____

_____

_____

_____

_____6

68) If you have an area of expertise, write up a short guide with tips and tricks as well as websites that will be helpful and hand it out to people (or give it away online). If at all possible, tie your information in to your BIZ OP business. But even if you can't, since it's your publication, you can introduce your BIZ OP business site complete with your domain name or Biz Op URL.

Date, Action & Results

_____

_____

_____

_____

_____

_____

69) Go to yard sales and visit with the people there. Ask them if they are interested in a way to make some extra money. Since they're doing a yard sale, the answer will be YES! Give them a flyer so they can check out your website later.

YARD SALE

Date, Action & Results

_____

_____

_____

_____

_____

POWER MODULE # 17

The Art Of Listening

You've learned a lot about what you are supposed to *say* as you are presenting your business to people. I haven't talked very much about *listening*. We're going to now, because being a good listener is just as important, if not more important, than knowing what to say. If you don't know where a person is really coming from, how are you going to know the right things to say to them? That comes from listening!

Mastering the art of listening will put you ahead of 90% of the people in business. **Do you know how to really listen?** 20% of your time in conversation should be spent asking and answering questions. The other 80% should be spent listening to what the person is saying and not saying.

You can learn more by listening, than you ever can by talking. Talk and you lose. Listen and you win.

Lots of people working to build a business do a lot of telling and selling. They spend lots of time talking about their company and their products, instead of asking questions and finding out what the prospects' interests really are. *Your prospect will tell you everything you need to know if you'll just listen.*

Learn how to read body language. Learn how to tell people's energy. You can learn everything you want to know about a person in the first minute or so if you learn how to do it.

Prospects love to feel listened to. Being listened to makes people feel special. Are you a good listener, or do you interrupt so that you feel better about yourself? Most people don't have someone to listen to them. When they find that, it opens their minds to the person who is listening to them. Listen without judgment and criticism. It will give your contacts a level of trust in you that will open their minds. Listening is critical to developing a valuable business relationship. Some good questions are:

- How are you feeling about your future?
- Are you living the life you want to live?

- What makes you interested in a business? (if they're listening to you, they have some level of interest.)
- What would you like your life to be like?

Find out what they want and need. That's the only way to help them see your business is the answer to those needs and wants.

If you don't listen well, you'll miss great opportunities. Developing your listening skills is critical to your building a successful business.

When you are talking to someone, really listen to them. Don't be thinking about what you are going to say next. Make sure you hear what the person is saying, not just what you think you are going to hear. There is usually a tremendous difference. You're going to have to teach yourself to master the art of listening.

Concentrate. Don't hear just what they are saying. Watch their body language. What are their eyes saying? What are they NOT saying? That will tell you just as much as what they ARE saying. Listen below the surface. Listen affirmatively. Affirmative listening is listening <u>for</u> – not just listening to. You're listening for what you need to know. Affirmative listening really connects you to the person you're listening to.

There are a lot of good books about listening. Go get one of them. Read it. Study it. Make it a part of you. It will not only help you build your business. It will help you in every area of your life – in every relationship in your life.

Make use of questions. Say things like:

- Can you say more about that?
- What do you mean by that?
- Tell me more...

Mastering the art of listening takes commitment to change. It means making a commitment to really pay attention to the person you are listening to. They will tell you what you need to know.

You already have a pretty good idea of whether you are a good listener or not. Just ask yourself honestly. If there is massive room for improvement – get with it! Your future depends on it!

The light burned late into the night. Finally, Jerry stopped.

Frustrated at his own limitations and inability to draw new characters, he quit.

But only temporarily...

After this latest futile attempt to birth a new comic strip, Jerry knew he needed help. Flicking the overhead lights off and heading to bed, he decided that come morning's light, he'd call Jim.

Maybe together they could do what he could not do alone.

"Jim? Hey, I've got an idea for a new strip. However, everything I draw looks like something I've done before. Can you look at it? Give me some pointers? Great! Thanks. I'd appreciate it. I want to do something new and I think together we'd make a great team."

The word **together**, had proved to be the winning combination for Jerry in the past. He and Rick Kirkman created a huge success with their comic strip, *BABY BLUES.*

"Now," Jerry wondered, *"could Jim and I connect to produce another winning strip?"* The partnership, if it worked, could breathe new life into both their careers *and* their creativity.

The word **together**, was confirmed again to be a winning combination. Once more, Jerry was right to team up with someone else.

Both artists, though not strangers in the comic strip world, desired to bring new life into their careers. Yet neither had the right touch *alone.*

Jerry, author of the popular strip *Baby Blues* and former creator of *NANCY*, writes; Jim Borgman, (whose previous success lies in American editorial and political cartoons) *draws* the cartoons. **Together**, they provide a worldwide readership the opportunity to laugh.

If you've ever been a teenager or parented teens, you will relate to the high school characters in their comic strip *ZITS*. These characters amuse, frustrate, charm, and entertain their bewildered parents. Common themes of girl/boy friends, braces, term papers, and driving licenses, compete with such serious subjects as breast cancer, college exams, and speeding tickets.

ZITS is truly a success in the comic strip world. While only 200 newspapers picked up the *ZITS* debut in 1997, today in 2008, over 1,500 papers feature its humorous look at life with teens!

What would have happened if Jerry had quit and put aside his dream?

What if he had shelved his attempts and never made that phone call to Jim?

A world full of laughter would not exist for readers everywhere. Their success would not have happened. And Jerry's dreams would have been lost.

In today's world where tragedy and heartache can be overwhelming, it is so refreshing to flip open the newspaper and laugh. Recognizing yourself or your teens in *ZITS* can give a much-needed chuckle to many households.

Don't be ashamed of the fact you need help -- we all do. Maybe the answer to overcoming the obstacles in your life is a working partner. Maybe you just need someone who will work with you, bounce ideas around, and give you needed feedback. Perhaps you need a partnership so that together, your talents fulfill the other's talents.

Sometimes, it takes a team of two (or more) to bring dreams into reality.

I hope you will remember Jerry and Jim as you go throughout your day. Take a step (or two) toward your passion and be sure to include someone else along the way! You'll both be glad you did.

The way a team plays as a whole determines its success. You may have the greatest bunch of individual stars in the world, but if they don't play together, the club won't be worth a dime.

~Babe Ruth

70) If you get chain letters through snail mail, send them a VIP Invitation about BIZ OP. They already know how to advertise since they're doing it through chain letters, so get them involved in something legitimate that would be even better!

Date, Action & Results

_____

_____

_____

_____

_____

_____

_____

71) Speak to everyone you see trying to raise funds. Ask them about their cause. Then tell them you work with a company that can help them raise funds (Most companies have a fundraising component now). Ask for their name and email address. Let them know you will send them info by email. Be sure to tell them your name so they will recognize your email.

Date, Action & Results

_____

_____

_____

_____

_____

72) Reply to other people's ads and let them know about your Biz Op. There are thousands of ads online that you can reply to. View the person's ad, then copy down their email address. Use a subject line such as, "About Your Ad" or "I'm responding to your ad."

Date, Action & Results

---

73) As you use your BIZ OP products more and more you won't be able to resist telling friends and family about it. Let it come up naturally in conversation. Your BIZ OP is a wonderful gift to be able to give, especially to those you love and care about. Consider it as such and your excitement and enthusiasm will be contagious.

Date, Action & Results

POWER MODULE # 18

The Rejection Missile!

Let's talk a little reality today. You obviously see the value and beauty of your business or you wouldn't have gotten involved – and you certainly wouldn't be going through this book. Wouldn't it be nice if everyone could see it – if everyone could be as excited as you are about your opportunity? Yes it would. But don't count on it happening. *That is reality*.

Building your own business is fun and rewarding but eventually all of us are faced with certain widespread and universal challenges. *No matter how long you're involved with your business, and no matter how successful you become, there is always the possibility you will be temporarily shot down by the most prevalent and dangerous weapon of all – the Rejection Missile.* It can, and will, strike anytime, rendering us virtually immobile, thus destroying our enthusiasm and excitement, which are the essential qualities for success.

Everyone faces rejection in life, but what makes our form of rejection so devastating is that it often comes from the very people we most love and respect: our spouse, our parents, our best friends and business associates. ***It's a fact that rejection causes more people to fail in this business than any other factor.***

So what do you do? *First, realize it will not all be about rejection.* You WILL find friends, family, business associates and casual acquaintances who will be eager to talk with you about what you're doing; they'll have an open mind and they'll be eager to join your company. But it's those very first "No's" that can be the hardest to take. That's what we want to prepare you for. That way it won't be able to destroy you. You'll be ready for it if it happens.

The way to deal with rejection is to *CHOOSE to allow it to motivate you to succeed. Turn your battles into a motivational force and let that force propel you through those early rejections.*

Let's look at this... It really is true that a "no, thank you" is not a personal rebuff. A waitress pouring coffee in a coffee shop might be told, "no, thanks" by one, "no more for now," by another. She might be told, "I have plenty, thanks", or even "I don't like coffee." But none of these responses sends her running to the lady's room in tears because all her customers rejected her. And yet that is comparable to what happens to some people building a business. They take "No," however it is said, too personally. *Think of sharing your business as a sifting process.* Like the waitress walking around with a coffeepot, we are merely searching for those who WOULD like to have what we have to offer. Accepting "No" is merely part of the process of finding those who say "Yes."

You know, often the mere fear and anticipation of rejection will keep some new business builders at home. *Fear of getting started is the primary reason for failure.* It is an obvious, but unspoken, phenomenon. You might hide behind the need to learn more, or you want to understand your company and products better. You figure if you don't talk to anyone, you can't be rejected – right? You also can't build a business and make any money. You'll go weeks or months doing this "busywork," then decide your business just doesn't work.

The reason will probably be clear to everyone but you. The mere anticipation of rejection leads to non-activity, a certain road to failure. In traditional business, things may just happen, but in your own business, success comes to those who MAKE THINGS HAPPEN!

We've already talked about your **immediate goals and your long-term goals**. Let your goals be foremost in your mind. "See" them on a daily, hourly basis. Let your dreams and your determination carry you beyond the rejection missile. Know that it is going to happen. Accept that it is going to happen. Make it your friend instead of your enemy. Know it will make you stronger. Know it will help you surround yourself only with people who want to change their lives. Know that it is these people who are going to help you achieve the financial independence you want for your life.

Be sure you make the numbers work for you. If you only contact a few people, the act of rejection by those few becomes bigger than life. If you contact a few dozen people each week, rejection is no problem because someone will always get involved. Remember this law of balance: <u>increase the number of approaches and decrease the impact of rejection.</u>

One final thought. Think about these people who are rejecting you and your business. Are they wildly successful? Do they have true financial independence? Are they living the kind of life you dream about? Then why would you really care what they think? Whatever it is they are doing sure isn't working! File them away for future contact and move on! Don't let them defeat you!! Show them they should have listened to you in the first place!!

Ooops! I just thought the last paragraph was my final thought. ***My actual final thought is to tell you to call someone you know who is also working to change their life.*** It might be your Sponsor; it might be someone else. When the rejection missile has landed on your head and heart, and you're wondering what in the world you're doing, call someone. They've probably been hit by the rejection missile, too. They can laugh with you, cry with you, and help you keep moving.

Let's make the numbers work for you. Who have you contacted TODAY??

_____

_____

_____

_____

_____

_____

_____

_____

_____

_____

The first pictures impressed me the most. Extraordinarily detailed, the black and white steam train with majestic trees along the train track transported me to another time. It was so realistic; I could feel the train's rumble and smell the steam. The next photo of a lighthouse streaming its saving light through dense fog made me feel safe. The lighthouse stood as they all do, outcropped on solid rock with crashing waves. Yet the next picture mesmerized me even more...a faintly colorized old-fashioned water mill, complete with a young boy playing in the water and the water itself reflecting the wooden wheel.

What makes these images even more amazing than their artistic and realistic depictions are how they were made and the man behind the talent! In the USA, think 1921...the era of flappers, the jazz age, the Charleston...and the birth of Paul Smith.

Come with me and witness a man with an extraordinary heart AND gift.

"I can't go to school but that doesn't mean I can't learn," thought Paul. *"I know my body is not like the others' but I bet I can do something. I just don't know what yet."*

"A typewriter? For me? I can't read and I only have one hand that works. What will I do with it?" Speech was very difficult for Paul. Smiling his thanks, his face beamed as an idea formed in his mind. *"Wonder if I can type what I see? Wonder if I can paint with this typewriter? Can I make my memories?"* Paul eagerly looked down at the blank paper as a canvas and the typewriter as his brushes.

Using his crippled left hand to steady his unpredictable right hand, Paul Smith, born with spastic cerebral palsy, began an artistic career that would span *seven* decades.

Creating thousands of pictures with his typewriter, he mastered shadows, reflections and color. Unable to push down two keys at the same time, Paul most often "locked" the shift key and used the symbols over the numbers...the majority of his pictures are comprised of only the symbols @ # $ % ^ & * ( ) _ . (The link to his website is at the bottom of this page.)

Over the years, Paul's art has graced the walls of Mother Teresa and U.S. President Franklin D. Roosevelt, as well as hundreds of average people whose names no one would recognize.

Paul lived to give.

He joked, laughed, travelled, and loved life with his family. His parents, unlike many of that era, refused to give up their son to an institution and refused to give up on his abilities.

Not using his disabilities as an excuse, Paul taught himself art *and* chess. He became an intense opponent on the chessboard. He'd rather play chess than nearly anything else.

With no formal education and a medical diagnosis that would overwhelm many people, Paul decided as a boy to make the most of what he could do. He could make and give art. He could laugh and joke. He could enjoy people. He could enjoy his life and he could truly live!

Live is exactly what Paul did - every day for 85 years.

"Friends say Smith was uncomfortable being held up as a model for others with disabilities. He never wanted anyone to feel inadequate because they couldn't do what he did. He (just) wanted people to use their gift."

I am humbled by the sincerity with which Paul lived his life. His pictures are incredible. I need his passion to live my dreams. I need his kind of acceptance to give what I can and not compare my work to others.

Today as you live your life and work toward you dreams, remember Paul and his parents. His parents believed in him. Paul was a remarkable man who typed his heart and then offered it up for the world to see.

P.S. Paul's art can be seen at www.paulsmithfoundation.org.

74) When you speak to people, leave the hype behind. Keep it simple and honest. Focus on the other person. Talk about the solution to their problem, not on how much money they can make. Suggested text: Let me help you make money to get through these tough times. It's simply not too good to be true. This says it all (list your domain name or URL or create a text link.

(A text link can be created by highlighting text, then clicking on the link icon of your email client and typing in your complete URL address – be sure to include http://.)

Date, Action & Results

_____

_____

_____

_____

_____

_____

75) Consider sending out email messages to the same person every day for 4 weeks. Share email addresses/leads with your downline. Most people will not join a business the first time they see an email. They still might not if it keeps coming from the same person. But if the same email comes from different people, more people respond.

Date, Action & Results

_____

_____

_____

_____

_____

76) Use your favorite search engine and search for "paid to read" sites. This is a pretty inexpensive way to advertise as you can find sites that give packages out starting at a dollar or two that include links and banners.

Date, Action & Results

_____

_____

_____

_____

_____

77) Find the Farmer's Markets, Flea Markets, etc. in your area. For a small fee, you can setup a table to promote your business, products and services. It's a great way to meet people!

Date, Action & Results

_____

_____

_____

_____

_____

POWER MODULE # 19

Avoiding The Management Trap!

Here's something that trips up a lot of home-based business owners. You've probably got several team members by now. *It is never too early to learn the lesson we're about to share with you!*

Building a successful business should be based on a team-building philosophy rather than a supervisory one. Perhaps the single most frequent cause of failure in any home-based business is the mistaken belief we must manage the people on our teams. **It's tempting to bring a few people in and then want to stop and devote all your time to making those few people successful – that's what I call the Management Mouse Trap.**

Let me quickly point out that there is a significant difference between managing and supporting the people in your team. Playing caretaker to your team creates a false codependency; doing for others instead of teaching and encouraging them to do for themselves.

Home-based businesses are as different as the products and services they market. You may have to lead meetings, or do 3-way calls, or a myriad of other things. Your entire company system may be based on utilizing a sophisticated internet system. Regardless, you need to understand the "Trap".

The Management Mouse Trap creates two serious problems for a business builder. First, it produces weak and lethargic members because someone else is doing their work for them. Second, while managing others, you are losing valuable time that could be more wisely invested in presenting your business to others – building your business even stronger. **Remember, new blood is the lifeline of any business.** Continually building your frontline adds to the vitality of your entire business. If you stop presenting your business before you are earning enough to live comfortably, then you lose valuable ground. And worse, since you're in a business of leading by example, the people on your team will do the same thing – creating even bigger problems for you. The bigger issue though is that you are setting up the people on your team to not do as well as they could, because they are following your example!

Supporting your organization, on the other hand, is part of the team approach inherent in any good business. It involves responding to legitimate requests on the part of any and all of your team members, or giving them encouragement when they are feeling down. In this letter I'm going to discuss the differences between creating dependency and reinforcing self-sufficiency. It is critical you recognize (and the sooner the better!) the difference between productive activity and ineffectual, time wasting practices.

Now, I want to talk about something right here. Have you decided what your goals with your business are – you definitely should have by now! Are you content with building a small business steadily, or do you want to take it to the TOP? Think about it. If you want to go to the TOP, then this letter is especially for you. Even if you think it's not for you – pay close attention. As you see your business grow, your dreams will get bigger and bigger as you discover the true potential of what you can accomplish.

Most of us come into a home-based business because we want what we can achieve through being successful, and because we like to help people. That's great, but it gets pretty tricky when you are trying to understand exactly what "helping" is. Too many of us find it easy to fall into the "Messiah Complex." You know, you want to save the world – well, at least all the people you bring into your business. Because you care about them, you are determined to make sure they succeed. It can easily turn into managing their business for them.

Here is an irony you will see played out over and over as you build your business. **Those team members who demand the least attention are usually the ones who become the most successful.**

It's easy to sign up a new team member, and then proceed to do everything for them. You make their phone calls; you print their business cards; you handle all their computer problems for them. They call you every day for simple questions they could get answered by reading the company's training material. They want to whine and complain about how "Uncle Johnny" didn't come into the business, instead of moving on to the next person. They always have an excuse for why the business isn't working for them. Your response is to work even harder to make sure they succeed. After all, *this* person *really* needs you. When you get to the end of each day you wonder why you feel drained and discouraged, instead of rejuvenated by a growing business.

You've fallen into the Management Mouse Trap. Your biggest challenge will be figuring out who is really going to build a business. To succeed, they must have belief before evidence. That is, they have to be able to picture themselves there and feel the emotions of it long before it happens. They have to be willing and eager to do what it takes to succeed. It is unnecessary to fall into a management mode when you're working with people committed to their own success. It really is that simple.

If you are finding this book helpful, you will want to get it into the hands of all your team members. But, for heaven's sake, don't buy it *for* them – let them know how valuable it was for you and see if they are committed enough to make the investment. There may be a few people you decide to buy it for, but that shouldn't be the norm. You can also make this book a contest prize – rewarding effort with the knowledge to create even more success! Find the people who are committed to doing what it takes, give them the right tools, and then let them go do it.

Managing is always a temptation. But if you are truly doing the numbers it takes to succeed, you won't have time to fall into the Management Mouse Trap. You might think it is much easier to work with your existing team than it is to go out and build your frontline. But because your team will do what they see you doing, you'll end up with a whole team of people doing this. If you spend most of your time building your business, so will they!

The secret is not managing your organization; rather it is finding leaders who will in turn find other leaders. Generally, leaders must be found; they can't be created. Many people have untapped leadership skills that aren't "found" until the timing is right, however. You just have to keep finding people who are excited about your business. The leaders will emerge if you introduce them to your company, and then turn them loose to build a business.

So what do you do?

- Present your business to the best people you can.

- Make sure they have done their Training and know their websites.

- Make sure they know how to utilize your products or services.

- Encourage them on a regular basis.

- Go get the next person who will become a leader.

JUST DON'T DO <u>FOR</u> THEM WHAT THEY MUST DO FOR THEMSELVES!!

How are you doing with managing your Team so far?? Be honest!

_____

_____

_____

_____

_____

_____

_____

_____

_____

_____

_____

POWER STORY # 19

"Isadora?" called her mother, *"are you ready?"*

"Yes, Mama, I am," came the minimal reply from the little girl.

The music swelled and the youngster closed her eyes. Feeling the music, rather than solely hearing it, caused her to sway. As one feels their own heartbeat, she yearned to move. She longed to give release to the motion that surged like blood within her limbs. Startled at her emotions, Isadora opened her eyes to find her mother smiling approvingly.

"You got it, Isadora. I saw it on your face. You have it...let's try again."

The music started slowly and built to a crescendo. Each beat of the melody beckoned her to move. Again, strong emotion welled up and threatened to crush her. Release through movement surged through her as Isadora lost awareness of time. This unconventional exercise for the times allowed Isadora to *"listen to the music with [her] soul."*

Isadora's mother beamed. *You are ready. You and your sister can start giving lessons. I am so proud. You have the makings of a great dancer."*

With deep exposure to dance, theater, Shakespeare, and reading, Isadora Duncan fell in love - in love with each of these artistic endeavors. She experienced deep pleasure in dancing as well as teaching others to dance. Growing up in poverty, she and her sister gave dance lessons to young girls – beginning when Isadora was only 6 years old!

Imagine knowing what you loved to do and being given permission to pursue your dream...even as a child. Isadora travelled and lived extensively in Europe, leaving behind her childhood San Francisco home. She shunned most things considered conventional during the early 1900's including proper education, marriage, and the formality of classical ballet.

Highly sensitive and unusually avant-garde for that time, Isadora is known as the mother of *"modern dance...blending together poetry, music and the rhythms of nature...She gave birth to a more free form of dance, dancing barefoot and in simple Greek apparel."*

A gifted and exceptional artist, she was the founder of three European dance schools which were dedicated to endowing groups of young female dancers with her artistic interpretations and philosophies. One group of girls, nicknamed "the *Isadorables*," even legally took her last name. The girls traveled and performed with Isadora, even though Isadora was critical of the commercial aspects of public performances such as touring and contracts. She sincerely felt such matters served only as *"distractions from her real mission: the creation of beauty and the education of the young."*

While we are many years past her untimely and accidental death in 1927, Isadora's influence on modern dance ripples out to us today. Popular literary references, musical allusions, and even Hollywood movie citations, keep Isadora ever before the public.

She looked at her culture and thought, *"People do not live nowadays. They get about ten percent out of life."* Isadora was definitely not one of those people. She lived fully and was ever present to the moment. She was determined to live with arms wide open.

Losing two of her children to a tragic automobile accident, Isadora learned to live through her grief. Losing another son shortly after birth also spurred her to give voice to her emotions through dance.

She could have retreated into grief. She could have stalled her dances. She could have chosen to still her forward movement. But she did not. She continued to dance, and to teach dance. By refusing to quit, she gave me and you the wonderful expressive modern dance forms that are enjoyed and appreciated today.

I am inspired by her uncanny ability to have lived life her own way. She repeatedly went against social standards of her day. When she felt something, she offered her life to give it expression. She understood that she was distinctive in her interpretation. Sometimes that exclusive attitude was her downfall, as she often lived misunderstood and criticized. However, for those people who opened their hearts to new "modern" methods, she was inspirational and refreshing.

I dare you to open your mind and heart to new ideas. I dare you to be like Isadora and refuse to conform. Have the courage to live YOUR life!

78) Get a domain name and start running free ads on the Internet. There are lots of places that sell domain names. Make it simple and easy to remember, i.e., YourDreamMachine.com, MakeMoneyWhileUShop.com, or CavemanProofBusiness.com. I noticed a huge difference when you purchase your own domain name. It draws much more attention. My favorite place to buy domain names is <u>GoDaddy.com</u>.

Date, Action & Results

---

79) Place classified ads in Free local papers (like Thrifty Nickel, PennySaver, etc.). It will cost around $25. You can place your ad in the Help Wanted section as well. Use this same ad in emails and online: Hi we have had tremendous growth and are looking for an individual with computer skills, people skills, and Internet access to work from home. We will train you and provide you with a personal mentor. Please go to: (your URL) to apply under the business section and watch your first training video. Once you apply, your manager will contact you within 48 hours to discuss compensation.

Date, Action & Results

"Barter if you have something of value to offer. If you are great with graphics or writing ad copy, don't be afraid to ask for a banner placement on someone's site in exchange for your services. As you are surfing the Internet, when you come across a site with a guest book or a blog with comments, be sure to let them know what you thought about their site or blog post. Post a link to your site and ask for their comments."

80) Purchase 2 or 3 magnetic signs to place on the side of your car with your Biz Op information so people can go to your website. The signs should also include your phone number so people can contact you for more information. Use a catchy phrase like "Finally a Way to Stay Home" or "I Get Paid to Shop Online: Ask Me About it", or "I get paid for being healthy". Be creative and catch people's attention!

Date, Action & Results

_____

_____

_____

_____

81) Send snail mail (an Invitation Card, flyer or letter) out to everyone in your address book. In today's world of email, a real piece of mail really stands out. Make sure you hand address the envelope so it doesn't look like bulk, junk mail.

Date, Action & Results

_____

_____

_____

_____

POWER MODULE # 20

Conquering The Big "D"

We've already talked about how important it is to have a great attitude in this business! It will either make you or break you. So what happens when you get depressed? *Depressed?* Surely I'm not serious. Yep. I am. If you are a human being, with human emotions and feelings, there are times in this business when you are going to get depressed; when you are going to wonder if you're out of your mind for trying to build a business; when you are quite sure you can't take one more person saying no, or not taking you seriously. You get depressed. You're ready to throw in the towel.

Let's be honest. Does everyone experience wild success as soon as they start building a business? Does everyone bring on lots of new members? No. Surprised I'm willing to be honest? Don't be. One of the things I hate about some Business Ops is that honesty is frowned upon. They tell you to "Fake it Till You Make It". They tell you to communicate that you're doing great even if you're not. I think that attitude is both ridiculous and wrong.

I hear from people who say they are trying this or that; advertising in Free places online; etc. but they haven't gotten anyone to join them.

The danger of focusing on the Internet is that sometimes you forget how to talk to real people. Let's be real. As the Internet grows the number of people vying for free classifieds, banner spots, etc. is only going to increase. At some point things might become saturated. Only very savvy Internet Marketers will be able to make much of a splash on the Internet. What does that mean for the rest of you? What does that mean for YOU?

It means that you are surrounded by people every day who need what you have to offer. Use the Internet but don't forget to be HUMAN! Talk to people. Carry Invitation Cards. Get people's email addresses and then send them an Email. This book has a multitude of ideas that will open the doors for you. You might fail if you focus on one to exclusion - I promise you cannot fail if you employ them all! Don't let depression derail your success!

Here's the first thing you need to know – EVERYONE feels that way at some point in time. It's just a reality of being a human being trying to do something that is challenging. No matter how hard we work at adopting the Law of Attraction, we're going to have a few days where we don't do very well. Here's the problem. If you just work at McDonalds you can still flip hamburgers even if you're depressed. I mean, no one cares if you're cheerful – they just want you to cook a good hamburger for them. But success in your Biz Op depends on one factor perhaps more than any other – a positive, uplifting personality and demonstrable enthusiasm and exuberance. So what do you do if your enthusiasm resembles the final dregs in your coffee cup?

Let's take an honest look at this thing. Maybe you are trying to share your Biz Op and receiving a series of rejections. Or you are sending letters and emails but not having anyone respond. If they are strangers, that's one thing. But maybe they are your friends and family. That's even harder to take! Or maybe you've signed some people up and they are still perched on the fence post like a sitting duck, instead of out there building their business the way you are. You know what? It's inevitable. All of that is going to happen at some point in your business. Accept it. It makes it a lot easier when it happens. There is nothing wrong with you. There is nothing wrong with your Biz Op. You are no different from a waitress offering coffee in a coffee shop. Some people just don't care for any. You are merely sifting for those for whom the time is right. You don't get depressed because all these things are happening. You get depressed if you choose to dwell on these factors and take them personally.

So what should you do first? Call someone who is also building a Biz Op! Anytime you are grappling with concern, fear, or depression please give someone a call! Your sponsor has probably been all the places you are going to be. They have felt all the things you are going to feel. They have

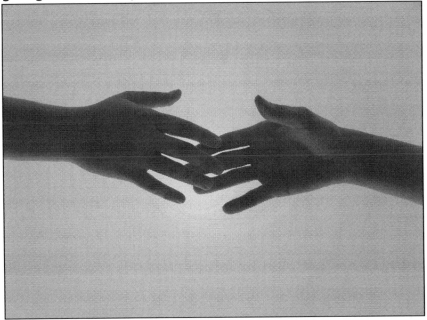

fought depression and wanting to quit. Talk to them! If your sponsor isn't very active, or is not available, track down other BizOp members. You'll find a lot of support!

Now, we're talking about depression because it is a reality – but the bigger reality is that you are going to have so much FUN working your business. You are going to achieve financial freedom and build incredible relationships with people in your organization all over the country!

Do you want to know the best way to deal with Business Building Depression? ACTIVITY! Yes, we know you may not feel like it at the time. ***That's the time to decide to do it anyway!!*** You are a very capable adult who has committed to building a business. That means sometimes you push beyond your feelings and do things anyway! Let us show you how it works. You're feeling a little depressed, so you only talk to a couple people this week. Both of them say no. Ouch! Now you're even more depressed! But what if you decide to talk to at least 20 people this week, or send out 50 emails? 60 of the 70 blow you off, but 10 join you. Now – are you caring much about the 60 who blew you off? NO! You're too excited about your 10 brand new business partners. ACTIVITY HAS CURED YOUR DEPRESSION!

*Depression can't withstand persistence. Depression will fall to consistent activity. Depression will bow its knee to the determination to **NEVER QUIT!!***

When you start to feel depressed....
* Vow to increase your activity, then DO IT!
* Call someone and share your struggles with them.
* Find the greatest motivational book or tape you can and immerse yourself in it.
* Call other people in your Biz Op who are achieving success and talk to them.
* Go back and watch your Biz Op presentation. It will reignite your dream and passion.

Your actions will follow the things you put into your mind. Depression will fall away with the ACTIVITY. And every day you will move closer to achieving the dreams that brought you into your Biz Op in the first place!!

I hated to do it, but I was determined to keep them safe. I had moved to a new home with a huge chicken farm across the road – not a place for dogs to run free. Our neighbor had a big rifle to protect his chickens and I knew he wouldn't hesitate to use it. My heart tugged at the sadness in their eyes when I pulled the gate shut on their new constructed pen one morning, but I was confident I'd made the right decision.

My two dogs definitely disagreed. Caspian, my chocolate lab, and Corrin, my huge black lab, stared at me through the slats of the pen as I walked away. As far as dog pens go, it was deluxe. A large 20 X 20 area under the overhang of my barn had been enclosed with 1 X 6 slats. I had scattered a thick layer of fresh smelling hay on the dirt floor so they would be comfortable.

They were clearly unimpressed. I, however, was confident I was being a good "dog mom".

Hmmm…. Caspian was about to teach me a lesson I've never forgotten.

When I drove up to the house that evening after a long day at work, Caspian greeted me at the car, his tail wagging wildly. I stared at him in astonishment. "How did you get out of that pen?" He kept wagging his tail, dancing in joy to be free. "And where is your brother?"

Wild barking drew me back to the pen. Corrin was exactly where I had left him. I turned back to stare at Caspian again. How *had* he gotten out?

Before I go any further into this story there's something you need to know about my chocolate lab. He only had 3 legs – losing one to being hit by a car the year before. It didn't slow him down but there were certainly limitations. *I thought…*

Determined to solve the mystery, I put Caspian back in the pen and hid around the corner of the barn. He waited only a few minutes before he calmly walked to the side of the pen and climbed…

Yes, my 3-legged dog climbed a 6-foot fence! He somehow managed to use his one good front leg to hook the boards, allowing his powerful hind legs to propel him forward. He reached the top, seemed to smile in satisfaction, then launched himself to the ground. He landed with a thud, his one good-leg not strong enough to catch him, jumped up, shook himself, and bounded around the corner to find me.

Corrin was barking wildly, infuriated to be left behind once again. He wanted out, but not badly enough to climb a 6-foot fence.

I stared at Caspian's look of smug satisfaction. I was impressed with what he'd done but I still had that chicken farmer with the rifle just across the road. My dog would have to stay in his pen.

With that decision... **the battle was on.**

To stop him from climbing out, I took 1 X 12 boards and nailed them around the top of the pen. Caspian stood on his hind legs, ate the board, then climbed out.

I changed tactics...

I replaced the 1 X 12, then dug a trench around the inside perimeter of the fence so he couldn't reach the board to chew it.

Caspian changed his tactics....

Instead of climbing up and over, he used his new knowledge of wood chewing to simply eat a hole in the side of the fence, large enough for him but too small for his brother, then climbed out.

I gritted my teeth and fought on...

Next I replaced the chewed board and lined the entire pen with heavy gage chain link fence.

Caspian ripped the fence away, wiggled underneath, ate the fence and climbed out.

Every time he would meet me at my car door, wiggling with delight that I was home and he was free.

But that chicken farmer with the rifle...

I put the chain link back in place, then secured it with 2 inch staples. I stepped back and knew I had finally won my battle. Not even Caspian could pull them out.

Wrong.

When Caspian met me at the car that night, however, I could tell his fight for freedom had cost him. Blood streamed down his chest from where he had ripped several teeth from his mouth in his fight to conquer the chained-link fence, and his face was cut, yet his wiggling body still expressed joy.

As I stared at my determined dog, my dismay and need to win turned to respect, admiration, and an acceptance of defeat. After all, he was at my car every night. He had never once taken off for the chicken farm. Caspian simply refused to have his freedom taken away.

As the warm spring air washed over us, I cleaned him up, then sat and quietly stroked his head. And I pondered what I had just learned. I had been fighting a problem with my business and had finally decided there was no answer.

Caspian taught me that wasn't true.

The lesson I learned that night is that there is always a way if I'm willing to keep trying, and willing to pay the price to accomplish my goal. If I wanted something badly enough there was a way to make it happen.

Caspian's persistence paid off. The next morning I took the door off the pen. Both my dogs stayed on my farm. They never bothered the chickens and I never had to worry about the chicken farmer's rifle.

And I learned a lesson I've never forgotten.

What do you want to accomplish? Are you willing to do whatever is necessary? Are you willing to pay the price? Only you know the answers.

82) If you sell on Ebay take advantage of the new format called "classified ads" where you can advertise any business you are trying to promote. (You CANNOT do this on the regular auction ads!) You are allowed to place a link or URL just as long as it relates to what you are promoting. It's a great way to advertise BIZ OP and use the power of Ebay's marketing reach. There is a $10 per 30 day fee added to your Ebay costs. You can also post it for 3 months for $30.

Date,   **Action**   **&**   **Results**

_____

_____

_____

_____

_____

83) Use pay-to-email programs like <u>Rent-a-List</u> (they have great support by email and by phone), Take the Internet Back (excellent support), Full Submission.com (check out their affiliate program). Full Submissions.com will blast your URL to over 3,000,000 places weekly as long as you display their banner on any of your websites, splash pages, etc. They also have killer page-view and banner display programs for cheap. They do all the search engine submissions for you so you don't get into trouble over-submitting. Their affiliate program is free and they have great support.

Date, Action & Results

_____

_____

_____

_____

_____

84) Don't overlook investing in yourself. Educate yourself with books on marketing and especially network marketing. Listen to or get a copy of "The Secret" and learn and practice the Law of Attraction. Become a better person and you will magnetically attract others to you and your business. *This may seem like the least practical suggestion – but in reality it is the most powerful!*

Date, Action & Results

_____

_____

_____

_____

_____

_____

85) Use a URL rotator (like PageSwirl) and include your team members' URLs who want you to help promote their BIZ OP. (Helping them helps you!) When someone joins your team, contact them by email or telephone and (a) welcome them, the (b) find out if they want to build a business. Add their BIZ OP (or BIZ OP domain name) to the rotator and then rotate the URLs about once a week so everyone gets some exposure for their BIZ OP site.

Date, Action & Results

_____

_____

_____

POWER MODULE # 21

Handling Criticism

You know that not everyone will be interested in the phenomenal business you want to share with them. People have their preconceived ideas -- and feel very passionate about them -- and sometimes you'll come "under their fire" because they have made a snap judgment. Don't let their ignorance and comments of what you're offering them upset you. But having said that, I also know it's difficult to do that.

You want to know one of the things you'll have to learn as you run your business? <u>How to have thick skin.</u> Let me share with you some of the things I've learned:

#1 - No matter what you do, someone isn't going to like it.

You may have a fantasy idea that you can make everyone happy. You can't. You may get dozens of emails every day from people who love you, your company, and what you're doing for them. Enjoy and treasure every one. Eventually, however, you will hear from someone who is unhappy, hates what you're doing, or just has an axe to grind. No matter what you do, or how you lead your team, someone isn't going to like it. Every single one hurts but you can learn to feel the hurt and then let it go, focusing instead on all the people who are happy.

#2 - You ultimately have to know your own heart.

One of the joys of leadership is that you get to call the shots. One of the challenges of leadership is the same thing - you get to call the shots. :) When you're the one calling the shots you can't pass off the responsibility to someone else; you have to claim it yourself, meaning that you become the target of attacks. You have to know your own heart. You have to know you're coming from a good place that only wants the best for people and that you truly just want to help people create financial freedom through an exciting opportunity. No one is perfect (including you!) but if your heart is in the right place, that can carry you through a lot.

#3 - Give yourself grace to make mistakes.

Trust me; you are going to make mistakes. I don't care how much you try to think through every aspect of something, you are going to make judgment errors and wish you had done things differently with your business and your team. I know you wish you could do everything perfectly. The problem is that you're just a human being. You will make decisions from what you think is the best information at the time - only to find that circumstances change, or maybe you just didn't really dig far enough to have the best information. You'll learn from it! You won't make the same mistake again!

The thing that absolutely won't help is to beat yourself up over it. All you do is paralyze yourself and you focus on the mistake instead of focusing on what is coming next and how you can do things better. Give yourself grace to make mistakes.

You know, I told you at the beginning of this that I was going to tell you how to have thick skin. The truth is – I hope you don't... After years in this industry, I'm glad to say I don't have thick skin. I truly hope I never do. I would rather be hurt from people's attacks than become impervious and hard. I've got hundreds of emails saved from people who are excited about what I've done for them. I read them when I need to. Sometimes I get up and walk away - knowing I need some space to keep perspective and keep pushing forward. I might cry a little. I might work out a little harder to release my emotions. I might call a friend. Once I've taken some deep breaths, I come back and dig in again - committed to creating materials for people that will create success for everyone who desperately wants and needs it.

4 - Accept people as human beings

Most of the people attacking you are angry, hurting or fearful. They aren't attacking YOU, as much as they are coming from a place of fear or misdirected anger. They are angry with their own lives, or they are fearful of what will happen with them. You become an easy target because you are a leader.

Here's what I do when I get one of "those letters". I allow myself to feel the hurt, I say "I forgive you" out loud, and then I pray for those people - asking for great blessings to pour into their lives. It doesn't matter what faith you adhere to – this is a universal principle. It helps **me** the most because I don't carry any anger and pain in myself. I release it back to the Universe and keep trying to build a company that will help everyone.

#5 - Look for the kernels of truth

I've learned that while I may hate the way someone communicates, I can sometimes find a kernel of truth in what they are saying that can help me either be a better person or build a better business. Hey, not everyone knows how to be diplomatic. :) I can shut out anything they say because they're "being a jerk" or I can feel my feelings, forgive them, and then come back to the letter to see if there is something I can learn.   Many times I do.

So, there are the lessons I've learned. I hope all of you who are leaders or emerging leaders benefit from them!

When someone dumps on you, connect with something
that makes you feel good!

The year was 1964. The place was Tokyo, Japan. The event was the Olympics – he was on his way to run in the Olympics! Absolutely amazing!

Billy let his mind travel back over the years...he remembered how he started running in order *to run away* - away from sadness and anguish. Orphaned as a boy (he hadn't even turned 13), he understood now that he first ran to escape his loneliness.

Soon, though, he realized through running and running fast, he could run to a future – a future out of sadness and into success. As Billy grew, he remembered feeling good about himself as he learned discipline and self-control. Having no parents meant he learned for himself as well from the teachers at the boarding school.

Many of his friends never left the reservation and they succumbed to the prevalence of alcohol. The fact he left many talented friends on the reservation grieved him. Yet he vowed that one day he would find a way to reach them.

Billy graduated from high school and then attended college. From studies to the track, he ran well. Numerous first-places created opportunities for him. He truly was a blessed and thankful man. Even without a family's guidance, he had stayed focused. He'd refuse to give up.

He simply wanted more of life.

Then he proudly joined the U.S. Marines. As a first lieutenant in the Marines, new situations arose daily. He had grown used to dealing with them.

But this was something totally different – it was the Olympics!

As the plane touched down in Tokyo, the young Native American looked around. A language unknown to his ears floated around his head as he waited for the ride to the arena and his room. The other athletes seemed as anxious and excited as he did.

He just couldn't shake the deep thrill that pulsated with his every step. Questions ran through his mind. *"Can I compete well enough? Can I even win? Can I take gold?"*

For most athletes, this experience was a once-in-a-lifetime phenomenon. He concentrated as he breathed in the sweet Asian air. Alert and single-minded, he didn't want to miss a detail! He etched this experience deep into his memory to carry with him wherever life took him!

Billy Mills is an Oglala Lakota (Sioux) Indian. *"Billy's given Lakota name is Makata Taka Hela which means 'love your country' or more traditionally translated, 'respects the earth.'"*

Billy is the only American – ever - to win the 10,000-meter (6 mile) run and

only the second Native American athlete to ever win any U.S. Olympic medal! Inducted into both the U.S. Olympic Hall of Fame and the Track and Field Hall of Fame, Billy's running career saw him set world records in more than one event.

His unexpected, triumphant, 1st place finish in the 1964 Olympics stands today as the greatest upset victory in Olympic history. Billy was labeled the "underdog," and faced indifference for much of the Olympic trials. However, his dogged persistence on the track and great strategic run brought him much acclaim.

Billy did remember his vow to return to his heritage and serve his fellow man.

Billy co-founded Running Strong for American Indian Youth®, now a project of the Christian Relief Services Charities, where he serves as National Spokesperson.

"In Lakota culture, someone who achieves great success has a 'giveaway' to thank the support system of family and friends who helped him achieve his goal. As part of his effort to give back to the American Indian

community...Billy travels over 300 days every year. He visits American Indian communities throughout the U.S. and speaks to American Indian youth about healthy lifestyles and taking pride in their heritage. "

Running Strong for American Youth® conducts "*youth programs, food programs, seasonal programs, culture and language programs, women's health programs, as well as digs water wells*" across the United States. Their motto says it all: "*Improving self-esteem and the future for Native Youth.*"

Who knew that orphaned, poverty stricken little boy would mature into an influential, effective communicator and conductor of change? Who knew he would bring help and hope to thousands of people?

I close this tribute with two quotes from Billy himself:

"*The ultimate is not to win, but to reach within the depths of your capabilities and to compete against yourself to the greatest extent possible. When you do that, you have dignity. You have the pride. You can walk about with character and pride, no matter in what place you happen to finish.*"

"*I was constantly told and challenged to live my life as a warrior. As a warrior, you assume responsibility for yourself. The warrior humbles himself. And the warrior learns the power of giving.*"

Billy rose above his humble, bleak childhood to live fully and give generously. I think we should learn from his life and strive to follow his steps.

Think about your own life and your destination. Ask yourself, where do you want to run? Keep Billy's example before you as a mighty messenger of truth.

> The goal of many leaders is to get people to think more highly of the leader. The goal of a great leader is to help people think more highly of themselves!

86) Don't make your personal website a passive one! Be sure to add a "signup for free information form" on your website. This will give you information you need to contact interested people. You will build a steady and reliable email list. And since it's your website, add several links and banners throughout. Put a banner on every page.

Date, Action & Results

_____

_____

_____

_____

_____

_____

87) Get 250 business cards free (VistaPrint.com). Put your domain name on it so people go directly to your BIZ OP business site.

Date, Action & Results

_____

_____

_____

_____

_____

_____

88) Every time you receive junk mail with a postage free return envelope, take advantage of it! Someone has to open the mail don't they? Slip your business card, flyer, or invitation card into the envelope and send it back! You'll find yourself getting pretty excited about junk mail!

Date, Action & Results

89) Put your ad on a billboard or city bus. Thousands of people will see you this way.

Date, Action & Results

POWER MODULE # 22

If You Have This Under Control . . .

You've learned about a lot of things that are crucial to your success with your business. All of them are important. This one is **imperative**. No one can provide it for you. Only you can produce what is needed. Only you can make sure you have it. Only you can do what it takes to keep it. What am I talking about?

Your attitude. I'm talking about your attitude. You know, our attitudes are among the few possessions that are totally ours and can never be taken from us. Houses and cars come and go, but our values and attitudes are with us forever. It is only when we continually exercise control over our own attitudes that we can manage external circumstances. Real change comes first from the inside. Our behavior naturally follows.

There will be things in life that challenge our ability to keep a positive, good attitude. There will especially be things that happen while building your home-based business. Rejection can take a swipe at our good attitude. People not living up to their promises can deal a blow. Someone dropping out can be a bomb to our attitude. But only if you let it. It is up to you to determine how you will react to every challenge.

You can't successfully perform the tasks necessary to succeed when you are depressed, especially in a business in which success results more often from attitude than ability. Many people fail simply because of their attitudes. It is virtually impossible to get people to join you in building your business if you don't show them enthusiasm. You can't expect others to join you if it is obvious to them you are less than satisfied. Remember, enthusiasm is contagious.

I've talked about reading, listening to tapes, etc. It is so key to your success. Let me give you something to think about. This was written by Charles Swindoll, a best selling author.

"The longer I live, the more I realize the impact of attitude on life. Attitude, to me, is more important than facts. It is more important than the past,

than education, than money, than circumstances, than failures, than successes, than what other people think or say or do. It is more important than appearance, giftedness, or skill…

"The remarkable thing is that we have a choice every day regarding the attitude we will embrace for that day. We cannot change our past; we cannot change the fact that people will act in a certain way. We cannot change the inevitable. The only thing we can do is play on the string we have, and that is our attitude. I'm convinced that life is 10% what happens to me and 90% how I react to it. And so it is with you. We are in charge of our attitudes."

Your attitude is truly up to you. What is it going to be today?! This is so important I want you to write about it. How's your attitude? What do you need to change your attitude about?

_____

_____

_____

_____

_____

_____

_____

_____

_____

_____

The alarm rang out, shattering the sleeping peace of the household while two young girls dreamed of Olympic Gold medals, victory rose bouquets, and perfect ice-skating scores. The sisters knew they had to get up. *"Get up and practice, get up and practice"* the alarm seemed to say. Fighting off the urge to snuggle back down and NOT practice, Michelle lifted the covers as she opened her eyes.

Yawning, she stretched. The morning was still dark. 3:00 am was too early even for the sun.

Knowing she had a new jump and turn to perfect, Michelle forced herself out of bed and trudged to the bathroom. Her sister, Karen, had been up just a few minutes longer. She too knew they needed to get moving. The girls would practice for several hours before going to school. As elementary students, these early morning practices, while extreme, were their routine. They always practiced before school and then for a couple hours more after school.

Michelle worried, though. Her mom and dad worked such very long hours - sometimes two jobs just to be able to pay for all her skating lessons. She heard them talk about selling the house. She wondered if she was really worth it. Was she going to be as good as her dreams? Would she ever win an ice skating championship? Would she ever be good enough to be noticed?

She wanted to excel. Michelle so strongly wanted to be good that she could "almost taste it." Yes, the taste of desire always stayed with her but she was so young and her dreams seemed far away. Her coach said she was good. And her sister was a great skater. How could they do everything they needed if they couldn't pay for lessons?

Shaking water from her eyes, Michelle dried her face while gazing at her reflection in the mirror.

Her thoughts ran something like this as the advice from parents and coach came flooding to her mind. *"You have got what it takes. Just be patient. Work hard. Never quit. Be willing to learn and take chances. Enjoy your time on the ice for as long as it lasts and be thankful you have the chance. Take care of yourself as you grow and never forget, 'it's not about winning or losing, it's about the spirit of the sport.'"*

Glancing up, Michelle saw Karen's sleep-tousled head peek around the door. Michelle yawned again. Locking eyes, the girls' mischievousness peaked, *"Race ya!"* they squealed, as each made a mad dash to the car. Another day dawned for these future champions on ice!

All of Michelle Kwan's ice skating dreams came true...and then some. While her parents did sell their home and struggled financially, eventually, through the help of friends in the skating industry, Karen AND Michelle received the training and opportunities they worked so hard for.

Winning nine U.S. championships, five World Championships, and two Olympic medals, Michelle holds 37 perfect scores which is the most of any skater! She competed for over a decade and is the most "decorated" figure skater in U.S. history. (Her sister Karen competed favorably as well. She finished 6th at Nationals in 1997, represented the United States in numerous international skating events, and won the bronze medal at the 1996 Nebelhorn Trophy in Germany.)

Michelle skated through injuries and criticisms, falls and misstep. Many of her wins came after she had less than perfect performances. Many of her accolades rest on the heels of mistakes. Michelle shows us that TRUE SUCCESS means carrying on in spite of imperfection and despite negativity.

Michelle is "grace on and off the ice." Her response to NOT winning Gold in the 2006 Olympics: *"It's not about the gold. It's about the spirit of it and the sport itself,"* she told reporters. *"I tried my hardest, and if I didn't win, it's OK."'* One amazing aspect of Michelle is that she truly meant what she said!

Her personal motto, *"Work hard, be yourself, have fun!"* gives her life a perspective that I admire.

I hope you emulate Michelle's stamina, grace and determination to try and try again! No one wins that many events unless they've tried that many more times and ***not*** won!

90) Place an ad every month with opt in leads. <u>Extreme Leads</u> has worked well for a lot of people. View it, not as costing money, but as an investment in your business. You need to get people to look at what you are doing or your business won't grow. Also, the cost is tax deductible. There are lots of lead programs out there so compare carefully.

Date, Action & Results

_91_) **Take out online SOLO Ads.** A solo ad is effective because they are usually sent to your prospect's main email account instead of the one they typically use for junk or wholesale safelist mailings. Many times these email accounts are never opened and the emails never read. There is usually minimal monetary outlay and the return on your investment can be enormous because SOLO Ads are slected, targeted, unique and they are read! _(Put solo ads as a search in your favorite search engine.)_ Many people have found a lot of success with <u>Rent-A-List</u>.

Date, Action & Results

92) Set up a website for your frontline team members. Include ideas from this ebook on your site so it's easy for them to find and use. Offer ideas on free resources. Post sample ads and email messages you and they have had success with. I think the easiest website creation program out there is Homestead. *You don't have to know HTML coding at all. Within a very short time you can create beautiful and powerful websites!*

Date, Action & Results

_____

_____

_____

_____

93) Send postcards via snail mail. Email leads at $1 each can be deleted at the click of a mouse and are gone forever. A good postcard that peaks the receiver's interest, and lays around before being tossed in the trash can be cost effective. (Alex Mandossian suggests not putting the company logo on this kind of card. Mandossian has an ebook costing $250 but gives away the first 3 chapters for free and it has a lot of information in it. MarketingWithPostcards.com)

Date, Action & Results

_____

_____

_____

_____

POWER MODULE # 23

Getting Past The Gatekeeper

As you build your business you're going to have to get past the gatekeeper. In this instance, the gatekeeper is the person themselves – all the conscious and subconscious barriers they have erected in their mind and heart that would keep them from joining you. Your introduction to the internal gatekeeper is always the questions and objections they throw at you.

You know what? Anytime you are sharing an opportunity with people you are going to be met with a lot of resistance. It's just the way people are programmed. Haven't you been taught from the time you were little that "if something sounds too good to be true, it probably is"? We know we were. Well, we're here to tell you – you were set up! Don't misunderstand us. It's good to be cautious; it's good to scrutinize something in order to make a wise business decision. The downside is that too many people miss out on something great because they are convinced it can't really be great.

You'll meet these people when you're sharing your business. Please understand from the very beginning that the people you are talking to are already programmed to be skeptical. They are already programmed to give you a lot of resistance. Don't let it blow you out of the water. Accept it. Then prepare yourself to handle it the best you can.

I'm going to give you as many possible scenarios as possible but don't expect to learn them all at once. Prepare for the questions you KNOW are going to be aimed your way. If you're ready – they won't throw you. You'll start to look forward to them because they help you sort people until you find the ones you really want to work with!

It's also important to not trap yourself with the belief you have to know ALL the questions and answers before you get started talking to people – that you have to memorize them and have them roll off the tip of your tongue. That would be a HUGE mistake. Sure, you'll be stumped sometimes. You may even get blown out of the water a few times. So what? You'll just come back, drill the response into your brain and be better prepared the next time. It's called "learning on the job", and there is simply no better way to do it.

People are programmed to automatically say two things. "No." And, "I'm not interested." These are nothing but knee jerk reactions. Don't take it personally. They aren't really reacting to you – you just pushed a button by asking them to do something. They responded from the programming that is engrained in them. It's not about you. It's not about your business! It's about them and their excuses. **You have the privilege of helping them move beyond their blindness.**

I'm going to present you with different scenarios. Your job is to read them over and over, until they are engrained in your brain and heart. It won't do you any good to have the perfect answer if you can't remember what it is. Your own feeling of power will grow if you feel prepared to handle how people will respond to you. You'll be more confident if you aren't afraid someone will ask you a question you don't know how to handle. Knowledge is power. Give yourself as much power as you can.

*** Now, it's important to know the exact answers will be as different as the companies out there to represent. You'll respond differently in answer to a question regarding nutritional products, then you will one about telecommunications. But not much... The basic answer will be the same – you just have to angle it toward your particular situation. Work with your sponsor, read your company literature, and work with your own team members. Between all of you – you'll come up with the perfect answers – using these as your starting point. Make sure you write them all down!

Okay, let's dig into this... What questions will be thrown your way?

1) What's this about?

This is the beginning of your learning how to read body language. Are they being rude, or are they really asking? You can tell by the position of their body, the look on their face, the tone of their voice. If they are sincerely asking...

"I've become part of a business that will generate financial and time freedom for the right people. This is about me looking for good quality people who want to change the quality of their lives. Is that you, _____?" Then,

pause... You're simply waiting for a yes or no. You just want to collect a decision. You get to pick and choose who you want to work with.

The person who asks this is often someone who is an A type personality. They come across as rude and abrasive, but they may not even know it. They are busy people who just want to cut through to the heart of the matter. You will often find men who do this with women – thinking they will intimidate them. If you're ready for it, it won't intimidate – it will give you a chance to respond from a place of power.

Another way to answer the question is to say, *"I've become part of a business that will generate financial and time freedom for the right people, so this is about me looking for good quality people who qualify for my time. Is that you?"*

You want to give a soft, non-abrasive comeback. You don't want to respond to them with their same approach. Getting into an argument with them will not benefit anyone. Smile, pause, and then take the power back. Type A people will respect you for it. If they're really interested, you'll have opened the door to take the next step.

What's the next step? Either give them an Invitation/Business card or get their email address & phone number. Personally, I would do both. They may or may not use the card. They're more likely to open an email from you, or take a call. Make sure you put your name in the subject line and mention you met them. Something like: *John Smith – it was great to meet you today!*

2) *Just cut to the chase!*

Again, this type of response comes from someone who is very busy – most often the type A personality. It can be intimidating, but only if you let it. Actually, these people can be wonderful at building a business if you can learn how to respond to them. Just smile and remain calm. You're the one with the incredible business opportunity. These Type A people are probably working themselves to death at a job that is doing nothing but stressing them out. You're the one with the power here! You have the answer to their need for their own business and residual incomes!

Say, *"Good. So you're someone who is very determined."* Don't take their attitude as a negative. Or… *"Great, _____. You're someone whose time is very valuable. I'm glad you said that. Let's get right into it. I've become part of a business that will generate financial and time freedom for the right people. I'm looking for quality people who I can work with to build a 6-figure income for themselves. Is that you?"*

Or… *"Great! You sound like the type of person I'm looking for -- someone who is busy and successful. I'll cut to the chase right now. I've become part of a business that will generate financial and time freedom for the right people. I'm looking for quality people I can work with who want to build a 6-figure income for themselves. Is that you?"*

If they respond positively, you only want to get their email address & phone number, and hand them an Invitation card or flyer.

Now, if this person continues to persist, and continues to interrupt you, you need to decide if this is someone you really want to work with. Don't drive yourself crazy. Take the power back by saying just 3 words. *"_____, take this card."* Then, *"Here's the website. If you like what you see, call me."*

If someone is just being rude and abrasive, let them go. They don't qualify for your time and energy. You're not begging people to join your team – you're CHOOSING who you want to build a business with. Take the "no" and move on – knowing that you're moving closer to the people you DO want to work with.

3) *How much does this cost?*

This one is fun! *"It won't cost you anything unless you want it to. All I'm asking you to do is take a look. If you decide it has value, you can decide for yourself what you want to do."*

Don't get pulled in to talking about costs because all it will do is raise the red "money flag". Money isn't important until they have determined if your opportunity has value. Let your presentation or your website do the work for you.

4) Is this a pyramid, a ponzi, or a chain letter?

This is a great question. I usually manage to hide my smile, knowing most people don't even really know what one is themselves. It's just more of that programming stuff happening. It's another one of those knee-jerk reactions. You say, *"I have a great business opportunity to share with you."* They immediately say, *"Oh, it must be a pyramid scheme, isn't it?"*

Don't argue with them. Give it back to them, *"Absolutely not. And by the way, _____, what exactly is a pyramid?"*

Most people have a misperception of what a pyramid really is. A pyramid is any kind of organization, scheme or chain, or ponzi where no products are being moved -- money is exchanging hands with no products being moved. You can be proud of the fact that most home-based businesses are so based in legality. And, yes, you'll want to have checked out your company yourself! You can't deal with this one if you aren't sure yourself.

Here's the reality though, most people who use that excuse are using it for just that – an excuse. What they are really saying is, *"I don't want to ask Aunt Sue, or Uncle Johnny to do nothing like this. I ain't gonna build no pyramid scheme."* Let's be honest here. Is this the type of intelligent person you want to build a business with? Probably not. Tell them to have a nice day and move on. The bottom line is that you don't want to waste time on people who aren't worth your time. You're not trying to sell people into your business – you're sorting, looking for the ones who are right for you.

But let's look at the other side. Too many people, thinking they were building a legitimate business, have out of ignorance participated in a pyramid scam, only to find their company shut down by federal regulators. They worked hard, only to have something ripped from their hands and now they are negative toward any home-based business. If they are interested, they are going to ask intelligent questions. This is where you have the time to provide the information they will need to make a wise business decision. Utilize all the tools your company has to offer.

Here's where you say, *"I can certainly appreciate why you want to be cautious. Here's all I want you to do. Check it out for yourself. Give me your email and I'll send you a link to the website."* Or, give them an Invitation card.

So let's keep going…

5) Is this legal?

Let's not make a big deal out of this. There will be plenty of time to provide credibility info if this is something that really concerns them. But it might be just a knee-jerk reaction. Let's see…

"Absolutely this is legal. Do you see an opportunity here?" Then pause.

The pauses are critical. It's too easy just to keep talking. Don't. Pause, and let them fill the silence. You want to see what kind of response you are going to get. Some people will roll right on with you because they don't even know enough about the industry to know they should be concerned. We'll fill in the gaps and give them the info they need with their training. But if they continue asking, they probably have a good reason. People are wise to be concerned about the legality. This is your chance to tell them some of your company's credibility factors.

List your company's credibility factors:

_____

_____

_____

_____

_____

_____

_____

_____

---

6) *Where can I document this?*

People are going to ask this question after you have presented your opportunity to them. They like what they see, but....

Ah hah!! Most of the time this is a trick question. The days are gone in most companies where you are making the presentation yourself. Almost all companies have wonderful websites that present the opportunity because the percentage of people who can give wonderful presentations is pretty low. You really shouldn't be telling them enough that they need to go document – not if you're using your business tools correctly. Most of the time you just want to get them to the website. That will be the documentation they are looking for – with all the facts they need to make a good decision.

7) How much money have you made?

Okay, this is a baited question – especially if you are a brand new member. Let's have some fun with it!

"How much money would you like me to be making?" Then be quiet. They'll usually respond with something like, *"Well, uh..."* Or maybe they'll give you some kind of figure. Whatever they say, your response is, *"You know, _____, I could tell you anything. You really don't have a way to verify it. The more important question is whether you see this as a business that can make you the kind of money you want to make. Let's determine that, and then I'll help you achieve those goals!"* Give them an Invitation card, get their email address & phone #, and send them an email with a link to your website. They have to really see it for themselves.

Always be honest. Don't ever lie to anyone about how much money you've made. Don't ever overstate how much money you've made, or over-project how much money you've made. Remember, it pays to be honest. **If you're doing very well, just tell them,** *"I'm living a very comfortable 6-figure lifestyle."* Or, *"I'm enjoying 5-figure results from the comfort of my home."*

Don't oversell your business opportunity. Don't promote this as a get-rich-quick-deal. A business will only grow if you treat it like one. Tell people their income potential is only limited by what they do, but that the results are up to each individual person.

Okay, let's keep going!

8) How long have you been in business?

The first thing you need to clarify is whether they are talking about you personally, or about your company. Once you know, you can answer. *"_____, I've personally been in business for _____. My company has been in business since _____. (This is where you can add in some bullet points about your company: How fast are they growing? How many countries are they in? How many members/reps do they have) Find out that information and then write down your answer:*

Once again, people like this want confirmation. They want to know if your company is for real. Use your tools. Send them to the website. They'll discover everything they want and need to know.

9) I want to talk to someone in my hometown...

This happens a lot when you're working with phone leads, or finding people on the Internet, so let's break this one down. Why do they want to talk to someone in their hometown? They want to feel a little more comfortable. Fine. If there is someone you can connect them with, go ahead and do it. But let's understand something. Whether you have someone in their home town or not, is not going to mean they are going to be successful. Don't spend a lot of time trying to track someone down.

What they are really saying is, *"I'm not sure I can do this. Show me someone right here who is."* Or they're saying, *"What if I'm alone out here? How do I know you can help me succeed? How are you going to support me if I'm a thousand miles away from you?"*

Say, *"What you really want to know is if I can give you the kind of support you need in order to succeed. _____, I am only looking for people who have the vision to earn a 6-figure income. Those are the people I'm going to invest my time in. Are you one of those people?"* Put yourself out there as the leader they are looking for. They won't really care if they have someone in their hometown to talk to.

10) Are you publicly traded? Or, Are you listed with Dunn & Bradstreet?

This is a very legitimate question. Check your company literature and find the answer.

_____

_____

_____

_____

_____

_____

Pause... *"What other questions do you have about how to make money?"*

11) Are you a member of the Better Business Bureau?

Check your company information. Again, what people are really asking here is, "Is this company for real? Is it something I can feel confident in?"

_____

_____

_____

_____

_____

So there you go... 4 more questions – 4 more answers. Do you see how all this is building on itself? Your confidence will grow in relationship to your knowledge AND your experience. I can give you information – only you can provide the experience that comes from talking to people. And you know what? You're going to screw up. You're going to choke when people ask you questions. You're going to get flustered and think what an idiot you are. So what? That's part of learning. Just keep doing it. You'll become more confident. You'll become smoother. Your business will continue to grow. Allow yourself to be human – you can't stop it from happening anyway!

Okay, let's keep going with this. I've got 2 more important questions and answers for you...

12) Show me a copy of your check.

Absolutely not. I wouldn't ever show anyone a copy of your check. If you have to show someone a copy of your check it means you are having to beg them or convince them into your company. And, by-the-way, knowing what you make doesn't mean they are going to make the same thing. They could make more, or they could make less.

First of all, it could be viewed as enticement by the attorney general. Don't ever show checks. Don't ever fax checks. It's really not about how much you make. It's about how much **they** are going to make.

They really are just asking for proof that your company works. It's another way of saying, *"How much money are you making?"* Treat it the same way... Go back and review the answer to *"How much money are you making?"* You'll know how to answer this one.

13) Will you guarantee my results?

Don't get caught in the trap of over-promising and under-delivering. When you're first getting started it can be very tempting to promise people lots of things in order to get them to join you in your business. So when you are asked that question, respond this way...

"Absolutely not. Will you guarantee your effort?" Pause to let them respond. Then, *"What I can guarantee is to give you 100% of my effort to help you succeed. I can guarantee you will have the training to equip you to do this business if you're willing to put in the effort. I can guarantee I am the leader you are looking for to help you build your business."* Pause again, and then smile. *"Are you ready to start putting forth the effort to build your own business?"*

Turn the question back around to them...

Never make any guarantees because you simply can't guarantee whether your prospect will put in the effort to succeed. Then direct them back to the truths of your company. Show them the potential of their earnings and assure them you will be there to work with them. Help them develop their own vision – they already really know it is their efforts that will lead them to either failure or success.

They will appreciate your honesty, and you will have established yourself as the kind of leader they are looking for to help them in building their business.

Okay, are you beginning to understand how easy this can become once you know the answers to the questions? Questions aren't scary things – they are opportunities for you to understand where your prospects are coming from. They are opportunities for you to sort easily and quickly – knowing the type of people you want to work with, as well as the type of people you DON'T want to work with. Questions are really little nuggets of gold. Treat them as your friends – they'll treat you well in return!

For good or ill your conversation is your advertisement.

Every time you open your mouth you let people look into your mind.

Hmmm... I definitely think that is true. What I am doing right now is trying to make sure that what comes out of your mouth lets people have a positive look into your mind! ☺ Let's keep going...

14) Why should I do this?

"You shouldn't." This really stops them cold. Pause, then say, *"If you're asking ME why, then you shouldn't be doing this. You have to know in your own heart that you should do this because I'm not in the begging or convincing business. This question needs to go back to you. Why should you do a home-based business?"* Turn the question back to them. Let them convince themselves. Let them decide for themselves if their WHY is big enough to propel them to success. You can't plant desire; you can just lead the way to their success.

Let's establish something now. This person has just asked a "Why" question. This may not be the type of person who qualifies for your time. You're looking for people who are asking the "How" questions. "How do I do this?" "How do I make this work for me?"

I want you to really understand something here. You can provide the answer to "How" questions. That's called training. Your company has it. This book provides a goldmine of it. What you can't do is give someone the reason WHY. The "hows" will fall into place if the WHY is big enough. It is people who truly understand WHY they are building a business who will be able to surmount all the obstacles they are sure to face. One of the very first things you should determine when you are talking to someone is WHY they are listening to you. WHY are they looking for a home-based business? You're NOT trying to sell them into your company – you're simply looking for the people who are the right fit. They should understand their own WHY before they are even presented with a business opportunity.

15) This sounds too good to be true.

You're going to hear this one a lot. It's another one of those knee jerk reactions. Here's a way to handle it...

"You know, _____, you're right. I felt the same way. But I have a question for you. What if it is true? Wouldn't you want to know you checked it out as thoroughly as you could?" You're dealing with someone of a skeptical nature. Let them investigate. Just get them to the website so they can make their own decision

"This sounds too good to be true," is a knee jerk reaction. Don't knee jerk back. Remember, you're just sorting, not convincing. That attitude gives you the ability to respond calmly in these situations. Sort. You'll find the people who catch the vision with you!

16) This doesn't sound real.

This is yet another question, but negative in nature. Just ask them, *"Why?"* Usually they will go to the old adage, *"If it sounds too good to be true, it usually is."* Use the "Why?" question to evoke the real excuse. Now you're simply back where you started in the last question and you know how to handle it.

There is another possibility though. When you ask "Why?" they may actually give you some real concerns; some things they aren't clear on; or things they just don't understand. Now you have something you can work with.

A well developed sense of humor is the pole that adds balance to your steps as you walk the tightrope of life!

If you haven't caught on by now... it helps to have a sense of humor while you are building your business. People can be ridiculous at times. They don't even realize how silly they sound – or how silly they ARE! Just accept that you'll run into a lot of those kinds. The good news is that you will run into ENOUGH of the right people if you are consistent in working your business – and if you have the knowledge to answer their questions and concerns.

202

With that in mind...

18) I'm too old; young; too handicapped; too busy; I'm on welfare, etc.

Sometimes this is just an excuse, but many times these are people who have tried and failed so many times in something else. If your intuition tells you these people could be great, then say...

"I'm too old." - You know, unless you have all the money you want & need, you're not too old. Why don't you at least check it out?"

"I'm too young." - Nonsense! You're never too young to take charge of your financial future. There have been many people your age who have succeeded in building a business. Sure, some people will be put off by your youth but don't let their ignorance stop you from building a business. Don't let your age stop you from doing what you want to do. You're getting older every day!

"I'm too busy." – Is that the way you want to stay? If you continue living your life the way you are right now, do you really believe you're going to be where you want to be in 5 years? If you want your life to be different you're going to have to carve out time to make it different. Are you willing to do that?

"I'm on welfare." - Do you want to stay on welfare? Is what you're doing right now going to change that for you? All it takes is for you to have the desire to change your life. Do you have it? If you passionately want to change your life, I will help you."

"I'm too handicapped." - The beauty of today's home-based businesses is that anyone can do it as long as you can access a computer on a regular basis. If you can provide the desire, I can provide the tools to help you make it happen. The question is; do you want it?

Whew! We're finally done with the questions. I'm sure you wondered if they would ever end. I hope you learned a lot, but most importantly, I hope you have more confidence in dealing with people. The most important thing to remember is that everyone is looking for a way to improve their life.

The birth of their son sent shivers of joy up her spine. Finally the long awaited day had come. She was holding her baby - her son. Sweat trickled on her brow as tears filled her eyes. Too in love to notice her fatigue, she knew the next few weeks would fly by as they got to know their little man.

"Greta, may I take him for a moment please? We just want to wash him off a little. You'll have him again very soon. I promise!" The nurse smiled a gracious smile and picked up the baby.

However, soon something proved to be very wrong as they started bathing Nick.

"Once they got him into the nursery and started giving him a bath, they realized he couldn't straighten his legs," Greta says. *"And when they started looking at it, they realized he was completely webbed behind the back of his legs."*

Nick Nelson was born with something *called "Popliteal Pterygium Syndrome. The most common trait is a web on the back of the leg, something you can't just snip off because it's packed with nerves."*

His condition prevented full use of either leg; on many days, he suffered excruciating pain. As he matured, he became confined to a wheelchair.

Now Nick reflected back on his life before his first amputation... he remembered dreaming of so many things: running with his friends, jumping off monkey bars, playing basketball and golf. He knew it was an impossible dream in his wheelchair but a very probable reality with prosthesis and his left leg.

He was also tired of hurting. His desires impelled Nick to make this choice - he wanted doctors to amputate his right leg in order for him to live a more pain free and more active life.

"'Sometimes you have to make hard choices in your life," Nick says. *"And that's one of them.'"*

After a successful amputation and rehab period, his left leg also began failing as well as hurting him. It hurt so badly that he just couldn't take it any longer. This ten-year-old decided to have his left leg amputated. That would mean two prostheses.

"Mom! MOM!" Startled, Greta looked into Nick's drowsy eyes *"MOM! I'm leaving now."*

"Nick, I am sorry. I was just remembering your birth. I was so lost in the memories. Oh, I love you and I think you are very brave. I am proud of you and you know I will be here; we'll all be here waiting for you the whole time. We won't leave. Dad and I – everyone – we'll all be right here. You hang in there. It will be ok...We love you Nick...we love you so very much!"

Greta watched through tear-filled eyes as the operating room assistants wheeled her ten-year-old son, Nick Nelson into surgery. His decision to amputate his other leg had not surprised her. How many kids have one leg amputated? Very few...and fewer still decide to have both their legs taken above the knee. However, Nick - her brave little munchkin - had done that very thing. Because it was his life and his legs, Greta and Gary left the final decision up to Nick. Supportive of their son in everyway, they knew it had to be his wish.

"When I get used to them, (referring to his two artificial 'legs') I'll have no regrets, and I'm glad I made that choice."

Nick is a young boy looking to his future with wisdom. He knows he has to endure much right now in order to live the life of freedom he desires. He has spent time in a wheelchair and doesn't want to live that way unless he has to. He has learned to walk several times. He underwent numerous surgeries and rehabilitation. He knows life is not always fair. But he also knows sometimes you must do the unthinkable.

Nick carries a remarkable sense of humor, style and a positive outlook. During a hospital stay, he wore a shirt that read, "Dude, where's My Legs?" He once told his mother his biggest challenge is *"getting motivated to finish my math homework."*

I truly hope you aren't facing any decisions as tough as Nick's. Nevertheless, when tough times do head your way, I hope you'll remember this brave young man. He knew what he wanted out of life and was willing to do whatever it took to get him where he wanted to go.

94) Use an AutoResponder to communicate with prospects and members (as opposed to one-time mailings). The life or pro memberships do cost, but you can earn back your investment in a few months. Another benefit of autoresponders is there is no problem with spam complaints because they all require double opt-in and they record and file each member's information. *There are lots of good ones out there but Get Response is my favorite! (www.GetResponse.com)*

Date, Action & Results

_____

_____

_____

_____

_____

_____

95) Be an example and use your own products or services. Set up a journal page on one of your websites and notate your experiences and benefits. It will encourage others to follow your example!

Date, Action & Results

_____

_____

_____

_____

_____

96) Wear clothing with your BIZ OP domain name on it (front and back). Wear it at your local mall or busy stores especially during holiday weekends. Just walk around and be a human billboard for your own biz. Watch VistaPrint.com. Every now and then they'll run a special for free personalized t-shirts (you pay the shipping). Use a catchy phrase that will grab people's attention and then be ready to stop and talk! Make sure you have a supply of business cards or flyers.

Date, Action & Results

_____

_____

_____

_____

_____

_____

97) Go to a local print shop and get a sticker made for the back window of your car with your domain name in it. Red lights and parking lots are now your best friends. Get blue (or an easy to see color) window stickers at one of your online stores. They are inexpensive and look great.

Date, Action & Results

_____

_____

_____

_____

Are You A Talker or a Doer??

As you near the end I want to give you a challenge. Only you can tell which one of these two people you are...

Take a deep breath and determine if you are ready for a challenge and some soul searching. If you aren't, don't read this. If you choose to read it, then read through to the end...

As I grow older, and as I watch people, I have learned there are two basic types... There are talkers. And there are doers.

Lots of people are talkers. They tell you all about what they are "going to do". They have big plans and good intentions, but all they do is talk. They're always going to do it tomorrow. They're always going to do it later. They're always "going to do it". Sound like anyone you know?

Then there are the doers. They might not talk about it at all - they just go do it, then tell you about it when it's done. Regardless, they **DO IT.** If they say they are going to do something - they do it.

No matter who you are - man, woman, teenager - the results of your whole life will depend on what you DO, not what you "talk about"!

Would you like to guess which group of people is going to be the one that experiences success in life? Success in whatever they decide to do? You're right. The DOERS!

I learned a long time ago that important things take tremendous work and perseverance. I also learned the closer you get to the realization of that goal, the greater and more intense the obstacles become. It's as if the Universe is testing you to see how much you want it.

One of my favorite people is AL Williams. Years ago he went against the tide of standard thinking and began a revolution in Life Insurance. People told him it couldn't be done. They said there was no way a country speaking football coach from Georgia could turn the Insurance Industry upside down. He listened, then went and did it anyway.

I am going to steal a concept he used during one of his tapes I listened to. Since I'm a good southern girl I'm going to "speak my language."

Be honest enough to acknowledge if you hear yourself in this...

Folks, I've heard it all. I've listened to so many people tell me what they are going to do. I'm going to make more sales. I'm going to get a promotion by working hard. I'm going to start my own business. I'm going to make better grades. I'm going to volunteer and make a difference in my community. I'm going to...?

But... I just got to do a few things. Just as soon as things calm down at work, I'm gonna go do it. Just as soon as I get things together at home, I'm gonna go do it. Just as soon as I get my desk clean and organized I'm gonna do it. Just as soon as I learn some more things, I'm gonna do it. Just as soon as I have some more money I'm gonna do it. Really! I'm gonna do it.

As soon as I get smarter. As soon as I get braver. As soon as I have more time. As soon as I get focused. Then I'm going to do it.

Folks, you're gonna spend the rest of your life getting ready. You're going to spend the rest of your life TALKING about what you're gonna do.

There's only one remedy. You got to go DO IT. Just go DO IT. Don't tell me about what you're going to do. Just go do it. What are you going to do? Whatever it takes to accomplish your goals. Whatever it takes to create the kind of life you want.

Just do it. And if you do it, and do it, and do it? You'll be exactly what you want to be. All your dreams will come true.

*Doggone it folks. You just got to quit TALKING about what you're going to do. You got to go **DO IT. AND DO IT. AND DO IT. AND DO IT.***

JUST DO IT!!

We want you to stop what you're doing and think for a few minutes - or as long as it takes. Then we want you to write yourself a letter. Make a commitment to yourself about what you are going to DO. Make a list of your goals and put them where you'll see them.

Here's something that will really determine if you are a talker or a Doer. Write your letter, then ask a friend to mail it to you in 2-3 months. You can put it in a self-addressed, stamped envelope they will merely slip in the mail. You'll be able to see for yourself whether you are a talker or a DOER.

(Write your letter right now!)

_____

_____

_____

_____

_____

_____

_____

_____

_____

_____

_____

_____

_____

Challenging you because...

I BELIEVE IN YOU!

Blue sky surrounded them. Wispy white clouds parted for them to pass. The whoosh of the thin air comforted him. Feeling free, he turned and looked at his lovely wife and their young son, David. How glad he was for their company. Smiling, he sighed. A sigh of deep satisfaction and anticipation seemed to originate from deep within his spirit.

Turning to tinker with his newest invention, Bill hoped to complete his "finishing touches" on this flight. Having developed an '"autopilot" for airplanes, Bill focused on the final touches of his invention. Too focused. He actually did not notice when his airplane slid into the identification zone of

Air Defense. He knew he was supposed to have prior authorization to fly here. He did not have permission to fly across this territory. He knew better. Today however, he flew haphazardly, too engrossed in his work.

Soon there was trouble.

The U.S. Air Force scrambled fighters to *"intercept and identify"* this violator of air space. As he recognized the Air Force planes, Bill engaged the plane to Auto Pilot, slid out of the pilot's seat and placed young 4-year-old David in the pilot's seat. Hiding down on the floor in the back, he asked his son to smile and wave at the man in the other airplane. Soon Bill Lear *"collapsed with laughter thinking about how the pilots were going to report this threat to Western Security."*

Bill Lear, we recognize as being synonymous with *"Lear Jet."* Yes Bill was aviator "deluxe" but also inventor "deluxe." Amazingly, this man had no more than an 8th grade education! Growing up, he did have a fascination with all things electronic!

To his credit are numerous patents and inventions.

One that surprised me was the 8-track tape. I remember in the 1970s being serenaded as one played in my car.

His earlier attempts at perfecting the automobile radio eventually grew into the Motorola Corporation.

He invented directional finders, air radios and autopilots for aviation.

When he released his radical business aircraft the "Lear Jet" to the Federal Aviation Administration for official certification, the test pilot made a critical error and crashed on take off! Two months later, with FFA certification in hand, Bill realized his dream *"to produce the first jet aircraft ever developed and financed by a single individual."* His handiwork was able to ...*"fly at over 40,000 feet, hit 605 miles per hour and outperform most military fighters."* The first year (1964 - 1965) sales of the Lear Jet totaled an amazing $52 million!

The Lear Jet became the ultimate status symbol for corporate and individual success. For decades, true "status" equaled owning a Lear Jet.

Seeing things that were not available and believing they could exist, Bill created the world he envisioned. Even as he neared 77 years of age and battled leukemia, he remained dedicated to the development of his latest brainchild: a corporate jet system, which he thought would operate at 1/10th the price of a current jet.

WOW! Without an education, Bill relied solely on himself and his active and imaginative mind.

I want to incorporate his tenacious dedication to my dreams. While I know nothing great is born without sacrifice, I will focus on my goals and dreams. I can keep trying and trying, and I know if I do, one day I will be successful.

You, too, can live the life you desire.

Maybe you don't have everything you need just yet, but I believe you can make a difference. I encourage you today to put one foot in front of the other and keep doing what you need to until you have reached your goal.

> "The first thing I did was go to the moms sites, like momclub.com and let people who were asking about work at home opportunities know about my Biz Op. I went and put ads in my local newspaper and weekly shopper. I told family and friends.

98) Hire a company that distributes flyers. The cost is very reasonable. Decide the area you want the flyer distributed to. Then you provide the flyers, the company picks them up and hand delivers them to the neighborhood of your choice. If you can't afford that – dust off your walking shoes and go get some great exercise!

Date, Action & Results

_____

_____

_____

_____

_____

_____

99) If you purchase leads be sure the lead source company includes date/time stamp and IP information. This is protection you have against spam complaints. Also be sure that every one of your emails includes a valid method to opt-out of your mailing list. If the leads have phone numbers, call them before sending an email. A possible script could be: "I understand you are looking for ways to generate case working from home. Is that correct?" (Wait for an answer.) "I've found this great business I would love to share with you! May I have your email address so I can send you my business link?" Then tell them the subject line in the email will say: "Information from ____, I spoke with you on the phone today" so they won't delete it. Send a very brief personal note. The important thing is to get them to your website!

Date, Action & Results

---

100) Put an ad in your local newspaper. It can be in the classifieds or a full blown advertisement depending on your budget. Promoting offline as well as online will have its benefits! Don't neglect other offline publications (professional journals, periodicals, etc.)

Date, Action & Results

---

101) Create a distribution list of your team members (to get them shopping or using your service!) and/or people who haven't signed up yet and send them "teaser" emails about a special running in your Biz Op. If your Biz Op doesn't send you updates, just watch your website and then alert people to great news or opportunities. This can be very simple if you're using an autoresponder that has Broadcast capability. *Get Response*

Date, Action & Results

_____

_____

_____

_____

_____

_____

102) Check out <u>Take The Internet Back</u>. I'm hesitant to add this in because I haven't used it myself (the reason it is 102!) but I had several people swear by it so it's at least worth a look! (www.taketheinternetback.com)

Date, Action & Results

_____

_____

_____

_____

_____

POWER MODULE # 25

Time To Take Stock

Well, you've reached the end of our journey together. Congratulations! This is also your day to be honest with yourself. I have some questions for you: (Use the space provided to make fresh commitments if you need to.)

•   Have you reached the goals you set for yourself in the beginning? (Go back over them...)

_____

_____

_____

_____

•   How many people have you added to your front line? Are you satisfied with it?

_____

_____

_____

_____

•   How many personal emails have you sent?

_____

_____

_____

_____

- How many Invitation or business cards, or flyers have you handed out?

_____

_____

_____

_____

- How many contacts have you made each day?

_____

_____

_____

_____

- Have you gone through all your company's training material?

_____

_____

_____

_____

- Do you know your product or service inside and out?

_____

_____

_____

_____

- Are you purchasing and using your product or service?

_____

_____

_____

_____

Okay, those questions should get you started. I strongly encourage you to – every 30 days – stop and evaluate your business. Come back to this book and review your goals and commitments. This is your time to analyze your strengths and be honest about your weaknesses. Where are you falling down on building your business? What areas do you need to get better in? What can you do to ensure you accomplish your goals in the next 30 days?

Once you have taken an honest look, now is the time to set your next 30 day goals. Do this on a monthly basis. We've talked about the importance of goals already. They will remain critically important as long as you are building your business.

- <u>What do you want to accomplish this next month?</u>

_____

_____

_____

_____

_____

_____

_____

_____

_____

_____

_____

_____

_____

_____

_____

_____

_____

_____

_____

_____

- How many people are you going to contact each day/week?

_____

_____

_____

- How many personal emails are you going to send?

_____

_____

_____

_____

- How many Invitation/Business cards or flyers are you going to hand out?

_____

_____

_____

_____

- How many people are going to be added to your team?

_____

_____

_____

_____

- What are you going to do to make yourself better this month?

_____

_____

_____

_____

Keep your business building simple. You're ready to create the success you dream of. All you have to do is DO IT. Be consistently consistent.

Right now you are in one of 3 places:

1-   You didn't reach your goals for your first 30 days.
2-   You reached them, but you wished you had done more.
3-   Your business is really taking off.

Today is a brand new day. What you have done before now doesn't really matter. You can decide now to reach your goals for the next 30 days. You can decide now to build the momentum you wished you already had going. You can continue the momentum you've built the last month and keep things rolling! The decision is yours. The actions will be up to you!

I am a big fan of working things way backward when I set a goal. The best way to explain this to you is to use an example.

Let's say your first business goal is to have 50 people you have personally sponsored. Okay. My first question is; when do you intend to have them? It's not enough to say you want 50. Give it a date.

Maybe your answer is one year. Okay... Assuming you'll take two weeks of vacation, you'll need to get 1 per week. **1 per week.** That's your first "Working It Backward Goal".

What are you going to do? Each person's answer will be different but let's say your plan is to:

-    have at least 3 people at a meeting each week (you figure you'll have to invite 10 to get 3 there)
-    send 50 personal emails
-    hand out 50 invitation/business cards
-    advertise online in at least 1 place
-    apply at least 2 of the ideas a week for that year.

Okay. What do you have to do on a **daily** basis to make that happen?

Drum Roll Please....

You're going to have to:

- invite at least 2 people a day to a meeting
- give out 7 Invitation/business cards
- send out 8 personal emails a day for 5 days, and then send out 10 on the 6th day.
- I think you can figure out the math on the advertising and idea application. ☺

Great! Now you know what you need to do on a DAILY basis to make your goal of adding at least one person a week to your frontline. Just for the record, I think you'll get more than one if you do this much but I don't think you'll mind *that*. This is what "Working a Goal Backward" is all about. Take an overall goal and break it down into daily or even hourly activity. That way you don't get to Saturday and say, "Oh my gosh, I have to give out 50 Invitation/Business Cards today!"

Of course, realistically you're not going to do that, so you throw up your hands, decide you've failed and give up. Or you just say, "Well, I'll do it next week..." and then repeat the same pattern – frustrated because you're not experiencing success.

Work your goals backward and then commit to your DAILY activities to make your dreams a reality. I believe you can do it!

POWER STORY # 25

The majestic Navy ship waited patiently to reach water. Dry-docked until its christening, the ship proudly displayed its name: USNS Carl Brashear.

Lauren nervously waited as well. She remembered the stories her grandfather, Carl Brashear, told of his time in the Navy. Definitely a different time in history and the U.S. military, Carl told stories of indifference, apathy and ignorance. Initially his skills as an officer and a diver went less recognized than other sailors' because he was African American.

Lauren looked over the sea, waiting for the U.S. Naval officials, dignitaries and family members to arrive. The waves gently rocked while she let her mind travel back in time. She heard the echo of her grandfather's story from a place deep within her spirit.

"...I was the son of sharecroppers. So, I joined the Navy in 1948, at a time when African Americans were few in the Navy. Initially I was destined to work in the ship's kitchen like most blacks on the ship; my job was to feed the white sailors. However, I had a dream. I dreamed of being a diver...the best diver the Navy had. The best divers went to Dive School and I wanted to attend Dive School. No black man had ever gone to Dive School, so I applied. I wrote a letter of application. When that letter returned rejected, I wrote again. That one rejected, I wrote again. And again. I had to write more than 100 letters asking for admission to the Diving School. I simply wanted to deep-sea dive. The Navy in 1954 finally agreed and allowed me entrance. Amidst much prejudice and hatred, I did graduate as a Navy Salvage Diver and I was the very first African American to do so."

Carl's dream had begun. As Carl lived his Navy career, he lived out his dreams.

When he decided to be a certified Naval Master Diver, he succeeded. He was the first African American to receive that certification. Lauren could not list the very long record of his accomplishments, medal, services, and decorations. The list seemed endless. Lauren did remember, though, the tragedy that truly set apart her grandfather from other men.

During a dive, through no fault of his, he suffered a serious accident. His leg sheered off below the knee, and forced him to live the rest of his life an amputee. When Navy officials demanded he retire, Carl fought and refused.

Carl still had dreams.

He had not fulfilled all that his heart contained. Struggling with an unfamiliar prosthetic leg, Carl had to re-prove himself. He had to prove that he could physically succeed as an officer, a diver, and a sailor. He stubbornly and faithfully worked relentlessly during his rehabilitation. Demonstrating his regained prowess to officers who doubted his abilities, Carl argued and demonstrated his way into remaining in the military. Not only was he

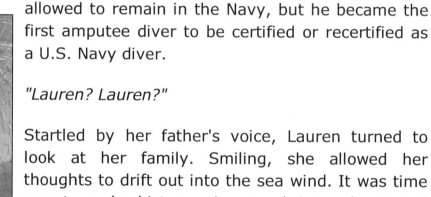

allowed to remain in the Navy, but he became the first amputee diver to be certified or recertified as a U.S. Navy diver.

"Lauren? Lauren?"

Startled by her father's voice, Lauren turned to look at her family. Smiling, she allowed her thoughts to drift out into the sea wind. It was time now to make history...time to christen the United States Naval Ship Carl Brashear...her granddaddy's ship.

Naval tradition requests a female relative serve as the sponsor of a vessel for its namesake. Proud to be the chosen relative, Lauren gazed briefly at the audience. Her eyes widened. There on the dock among Naval officials, and family members sat Academy Award winning actor Robert DeNiro. Along with him were other Hollywood notables. She should have known they would be present. Her grandfather's life was the subject of *Men of Honor*, a movie starring DeNiro and Cuba Gooding Jr.

With Cuba's portrayal of the determined naval diver, Carl seemed immortal.

He truly was a pioneer in the Navy and these talented actors showed great respect for his life. She remembered his thoughts about the actors' depiction of his life, *"'They will know I was one dedicated young man. I love the*

United States Navy and I set my goals high. I worked toward those goals with all my might.'"

Lauren knew her grandfather would have been humbled, honored, and proud. She could hear his voice, replaying his mottos..."*It's not a sin to get knocked down; it's a sin to stay down*" and "*I ain't going to let nobody steal my dream.*"

Through it all, her granddad never asked for special favors, he just wanted the chance to prove himself.

As she held up the bottle of champagne to strike and formally launch the ship, she smiled.

At the appropriate time, she looked first to the sea, then to the heavens and then to the majestic vessel.

"Here's to you, Granddad. I am proud of you...we all are. I now christen this ship the USNS Carl Brashear." Smashing the bottle against the helm of the mighty ship, Lauren nodded her head. She knew her grandfather smiled from heaven at the crowd and saluted.

Carl Brashear was not looking to make history as he proudly served in the United States. He just wanted to fulfill the burning dreams that lived within his spirit. He just wanted to live fully. Yet he lived determined to change history if that was required. He was willing to prove himself able and worthy. I am touched by his humble tenacity to be what he was created to be. I want to be more like that...much more determined.

Today as you pursue your dreams, remember Carl. I encourage you to work toward your goals with all your might!

103) Send Audio Emails – really stand out by inserting audio or video into the emails you send to your prospects. It's much simpler than you probably think – and much more powerful than you may realize. BYOAudio is my favorite! (www.byoaudio.com)

Date, Action & Results

_____

_____

_____

_____

_____

_____

104) Create Powerful Videos – this takes what I was talking about in the last idea a massive leap forward. Anything you can write – you can create an amazing, talking video for – in just minutes! Post it on YouTube, add it to emails, or put it on your website. If you want to stand out from the crowd, this is a great way to do it! www.articlevideorobot.com

Date, Action & Results

_____

_____

_____

105) <u>Tips on Placing Ads</u>

Here are some great tips for placing ads. "One thing does need to be understood when advertising, either you have to pay with time or money."

#1 rule. Do not over post... While it is OK to post to multiple cities at one sitting, do not post ads to the same city on consecutive days. Wait 3 - 4 days for your ad to drop off that cities front page.

Do your best to post in the appropriate category. Show the same courtesy posting ads, as you would expect if you were reading them. Posting in the wrong category is another form of 'SPAM'

On most ad sites you will get a **renewal notice by email** after 45 days (or whatever their basic ad length is), at that point you can just click renew on the email they send you.

Change your Headlines periodically. When people get used to seeing the same thing over and over they will train themselves to
ignore what is common. So change it up and make your headlines stand out without over exaggeration.

You **do not have to sit for hours at a time** posting ads. Find a site or two, post 5 to 10 ads, or set a time limit. Say 20 minutes a day. Before you know it you will have quite a presence out there.

"Ok, aren't you tired of typing out ads?" It's true I have placed 100's of ads, but in reality there is a simple way to post lots of ads and minimize the work at the same time.

(1) Type your ad, complete with 'headline', 'message', and link onto notepad or another similar program. Once you have done that, choose 'file' and then 'save as', give the file a name of your choice. When you choose the site that you would like to place your ads on, open your file. Most sites have a separate field for 'Headline' 'ad body' and your 'email address'. Some also have a separate 'link' field.

(2) Now copy and paste your information to the appropriate fields. For single line entries like your 'headline' or 'email address' and 'links,' if you backspace the last couple characters and then retype them, that information should be stored there for later use. When you come back to these single line fields later, double click on them and you should have a list drop down for you to pick from.

And now for a brief advertisement... Not about a Biz Opportunity - but simply a way to make a difference in the world!

I also own a company called Together We Can Change The World. And, yes, I do just happen to believe we can! Since 2001, we have been creating resources to GIVE AWAY to people. To do it, we have established something called 5 Million For Change. I challenge you to join, take the pledge, and use your life to make a difference in the world!

Together We Can Change The World, Inc. has created the 5 Million For Change Campaign to mobilize a force of good that will sweep across the globe and create true sustainable CHANGE on every continent.

It's not just enough to say you want to help create CHANGE - you have to have the resources and tools to do just that. The Together We Can Change The World Association has created everything you need - giving it to you totally **FREE** as our contribution to CHANGE.

---

14 E-books in the 101 Ways Series

More books through Together We Can Change The World Publishing

Powerful Movies & Songs

E-Cards

Personal Online Shopping Mall

Beacon of Light Cards

Prints & Posters

Will you RAISE YOUR HAND and become part of 5 Million For Change or 5 Million Students For Change??

5 Million For Change Pledge

I raise my hand for 5 Million For Change.

I will take time TODAY to make a difference in the world.

I will take time TODAY to do one thing – for one person.

I will take time TODAY to spread some love & caring in my world.

One thing – TODAY.

EVERYDAY!

Nothing is too small. Nothing is too big.

It is only important to take Action.

I will take time TODAY – to ACT – to create CHANGE!

www.5MillionForChange.com

www.5MillionStudentsForChange.com

I Believe
In You to
Create
The Life
of Your
Dreams!!

101 Ways To Promote Your Business Opportunity

Copyright © 2010 by Ginny Dye

Published by Together We Can Change The World

Publishing

Bellingham, WA 98229

www.101WaysToPromoteYourBusinessOpportunity.com

www.GinnyDye.com

www.TogetherWeCanChangeTheWorldPublishing.com

ISBN 0982717164

Printed in the United States of America